Lingerie

A Modern Guide

Lingerie

A Modern Guide

Lesley Scott

A Quantum Book

First published in Great Britain in 2010
A&C Black Publishers Limited
36 Soho Square
London W1D 3QY
www.acblack.com

ISBN 978-1-4081-2754-4

QUMLAMG

This book is produced by
Quantum Publishing Ltd
6 Blundell Street
London N7 9BH

Project Editor: Samantha Warrington
Editorial Assistant: Jo Morley
Picture Editor: Lauren Carley
Designer: Norma Martin
Production: Rohana Yusof
Publisher: Sarah Bloxham

Printed in Singapore by
Star Standard Industries (Pte) Ltd.

Cover image by Gregory Michael King, model: Dominique de Merteuil

Table of Contents

*Black bra by
Spanish designer,
Andres Sardá*

Foreword

If love is blind, then why is lingerie so popular?
Anonymous

I love lingerie. As a fashion critic and writer, I've always been fascinated by the sartorial story that can be told beneath the armour of street clothing. After all, slip on something super-sexy and frilly under a power suit and it's a secret little reminder all day of your inner femme fatale. For a hot date, a bustier with your favourite jeans and a stylish blazer sends just the right mixed message. And even when you're just lounging at home, few things feel as delicious as slipping off your working clothes and sliding on a sensuous silk robe. Few items of clothing can so easily create a mood, shift the vibe or set off shivers like the right lingerie.

The birth of modern lingerie

Although the first items of lingerie date back almost 5,000 years, it wasn't until the second half of the 14th century that shape-altering underpinnings became a prominent part of the process of getting dressed.

Farthingales, and later, panniers dramatically expanded the width of women's skirts, reflecting the importance of a woman's fertility; in those days a woman's ability to bear children was judged by the 'child-bearing' look of her hips.

The corsets that women wore even inspired romantic poetry. 'Off with that happy busk, which I envy', wrote John Donne in *To His Mistress Going to Bed*, immortalising the long paddle-shaped piece that kept the corset rigid and was slipped down centre front; its hidden nature and proximity to the heart made it a popular gift from men to their lovers, often inscribed with love poems.

In the late 18th century the women of Revolutionary France discarded most of their underwear along with the hated aristocrats of the old regime. Some years later, their Victorian sisters piled it right back on again. When Cole Porter so memorably wrote, 'In olden days a glimpse of stocking was looked on as something shocking', it was probably because it had to emerge, somehow, from under an average of 11 pounds-worth of other undergarments.

Lingerie as statement

In modern times, lingerie has come out from under wraps to make political statements (such as the alleged bra burnings of the 1960s and early 1970s), define a young person's coming of age (especially for many a young male obsessed with the Victoria's Secret catalogue) and even, as an eccentric sign of the times, (the Lingerie Football League in which women play full-contact American football clad only in a helmet, a few protective pads, and frilly underwear).

When Jean Paul Gaultier resurrected and amplified the 1950s cone bra for Madonna's Blonde Ambition Tour, lingerie completed a post-modern post-war circle. Other designers including Marc Jacobs and Dolce & Gabbana have been showing lacy slips as street wear and layering satiny bras right over snug sweaters for many seasons. Once a closely guarded secret, lingerie is now allowed to make its own high-fashion outerwear statement.

Why lingerie?

Sex today is so replete with repression, weirdness and fetish, that it's tempting to yearn for the 'good old days', when there was no embarrassment about sexuality and it was considered as natural and shame-free as eating or sitting outside in the sunshine. We don't put animals in lingerie (obviously, as it would make them look ridiculous rather than sexy) so why do humans wear it?

Probably because if we didn't have it, we would miss it.

Perhaps lingerie is similar to foodie culture. Food, like sex, is a natural human instinct. While a haunch of raw bison with a side of scavenged nuts and berries would probably more than satisfy the calorific requirements of modern humans, we've nonetheless chosen to 'play' with our food, experimenting with it and elevating it to an art form that includes strange and fantastic dishes such as Spam Musubi (moulded and canned pork shoulder, ham, sugar and salt, paired with white rice and wrapped in dried seaweed for a sushi-looking snack item), Avocado Pie (a cracker crust containing a layer of avocados, gelatine and sweetened condensed milk, and topped with meringue), Eskimo 'ice cream' (whipped fat, salmonberries or cloudberries, sugar and salmon, caribou or walrus tallow) and even just a good, old-fashioned ice-cream sundae, sweet, ethereal and of no nutritional value, but so luscious and fun, who cares?

I lingerie, therefore I am

Perhaps foodie culture is to nutrition what lingerie is to sex: a delicious, extravagant touch of mystery and mastery that makes sex more sensual, less prim and that much more fun. A naked human body dressed up in lingerie becomes alluring, teasing and far more delectable. From bodacious burlesque divas to soft-core porn queens, to any striptease artist worth her sassy salt, lingerie is key because it reveals and conceals, instantly transforming a naked body into something infinitely more sexy and come-hither.

The lure of lingerie is as much about sex appeal as it is about creating a fantasy. Lounging about in my white full slip, I'm a devastatingly gorgeous young Elizabeth Taylor as Maggie the Cat (in a *Hot Tin Roof*). Corset, garters and stockings and *voila*, I'm Mistress of the Boudoir. Wearing a white satiny slip and matching thigh-highs, and it's time for my own *9½ Weeks* striptease. Put on the right negligee, panties or bra, and va va voom, you instantly become a more alluring (naughtier, even) version of your workaday self.

'Sometimes I sing and dance around the house in my underwear,' Joan Cusack's character, Cynthia, tells Melanie Griffith's Tess in the 1988 film *Working Girl*. 'Doesn't make me Madonna. Never will.'

She was wrong. It does.

Lesley Scott, May 2010

Whalebone corsets from the late Victorian and Edwardian era

Lingerie from ancient times to the 19th century

Images from the earliest times show women wearing garments that resemble lingerie. The Minoan Snake Goddess proudly wears a corset-like garment while the 'Bikini Girls' of ancient Rome wear binding cloths clearly designed for breast support. In the medieval era, undergarments tended to obscure and flatten the body rather than enhancing it. Supportive, restrictive stays reached extremes at the 16th-century court of Catherine de' Medici in France, where a 13-inch waist was deemed ideal. At the same time, skirts expanded to emphasise the smallness of the waist; by the late 18th century, a host of complex underpinnings was required to support the fashionable woman's skirts.

Minoan Snake Goddess, *c.1600 BCE, wearing a form of corset*

The undergarments of the ancients: Egypt and Crete

Ever since women started wearing items of clothing for reasons other than the merely practical, they have indulged in lingerie. Fashion has always been a reflection of everything from the prevailing political ideology to social values, nationalism, tension between the sexes and other concerns that trouble the collective unconscious. More than 5,000 years ago, in around 3,000 BCE, high-status women in ancient Egypt wore body-conscious undertunics that fell to the ankle to show off their position in society. Slaves and people of a low rank either went naked or, at most, wore a loin cloth. In what is probably the first evidence of shapewear, the undertunics were often draped in order to highlight the waist.

The Minoans

A thousand years later in the Eastern Mediterranean, the Minoans, who lived on the island of Crete during the Bronze Age (5,000–1,500 BCE,) flourished as a matrilineal society. With the men mostly away at sea trading, the women ran things – in style. They wore bell-shaped skirts with multiple tiers made from wool – an indication of tailoring, which was considered unusual for the time – jewellery, turbans, elaborate hairstyles and what appear to be the first corsets.

The Snake Goddess figurine was discovered in 1903 by British archaeologist Sir Arthur Evans at the palace at Knossos, home of King Minos and the legendary Minotaur. She dates from around 1600 BCE and is clad in what could pass for a modern corset. The flounced skirt, which resembles a crinoline with an apron layered over it, is further cinched with a wide, ribbed, girdle-like belt. Evans conjectured that the belt might have been made from metal.

Girls rule!

What was interesting about the discovery of the Snake Goddess was what was not found at the site. There were no temples devoted to the gods, fortifications, and citadels, public sculptures of grandiose proportions, 'boastful inscriptions . . . [or any] clear evidence of a hierarchically-structured society ruled by kings and priests'. The typical signs of a male-dominated society were simply not present. The archaeological evidence supports the idea that women dominated Minoan culture.

Early Byzantine girdle made from gold coins and
medallions depicting the emperor Maurice Tiberius

The significance of the girdle

It is possible that the metal girdle had a ritual significance and was designed to protect a woman's fertility, the source of female power in a matrilineal society. The Snake Goddess's bell-shaped skirt also appears in the Balkan region in the Bronze Age, embroidered with images of the pre-Christian goddess Berehinia who was believed both to protect and to provide fertility. Like the apron of the Snake Goddess and, possibly, the metal belt or corset, the original purpose of this type of embroidery was to protect the wearer against evil spirits. The typical motifs – triangles, crescents, circles, stars and crosses, fish, birds, horns – were (and still are) placed at the hems, cuffs, pockets, buttonholes, heart and sexual areas, in fact anywhere where evil spirits could come into contact with the body.

Ancient Greece and Rome

The ancient Greeks were disdainful of people whom they considered to be barbarians and their way of dressing that revealed the body. The Greeks wore loose-fitting tunics, such as the elaborately draped rectangle

Cupid Undoing Venus's Girdle, *Sir Joshual Reynolds (1723–1792)*

The corseted, armoured goddess Brünnhilde

Aphrodite's mighty girdle

Some scholars believe that the girdle of the Minoan Snake Goddess was related to the magical girdle of the goddess of love, Aphrodite. She was used by Hera to distract Zeus during the Trojan War. In the *Iliad*, Book XIV, Hera requested of Aphrodite, 'Give me loveliness and desirability, graces with which you overwhelm mortal men and all the immortals.' Aphrodite obliged and 'loosed from her bosom the curiously embroidered girdle into which all her charms had been wrought – love, desire and that sweet flattery which steals the judgment even of the most prudent.'

Brünnhilde's girdle

In the Norse sagas on which Wagner based his famous epic operas, *Der Ring des Nibelungen*, the hero Siegfried was only allowed to marry the beautiful Gutrune if he defeated Brünnhilde, a valkyrie with superhuman strength and ability, in a series of athletic challenges. Using trickery, along with a cloak of invisibility, Siegfried was able to sneak into her bedchamber and remove her ring and, most importantly, her silken waist girdle: 'Thus was Brunhild subdued; after that hour she had but the strength of other women.'

of woven wool, known as the himation or peplos, measuring 3 metres (9ft 8in) in width and the height of the wearer. It slipped over the head and the top-most layer hung gracefully from the shoulders; the arms were left bare and the garment was worn belted.

Support beneath

Underneath, women typically favoured some kind of support garment; many were as keen on athletic pursuits as the men and, beginning in 776 BCE, even participated in their own same-sex Olympic games to honour Hera. Bust support was the top priority and was typically made from a long and narrow strip of fabric often using red kidskin or fine leather. Called the apodesmos, this garment later became more elaborate with embroideries of gold, pearls and gemstones; too lovely to keep under wraps, it kept its supportive function but operated as outerwear as well.

Roman underwear

Roman women also bound their breasts with bands, known as strophium. Mothers who were worried that their daughters might overdevelop made them wear a strophium, as did fashion conscious women who

*Women of
ancient Greece wore
loose fitting tunics*

wanted their tunics to drape as flatteringly as possible. Women also wore bust support during exercise, and a nappy-like pants that allowed for maximum freedom of movement, as evidenced by the athletic maidens in the Roman mosaic '*Coronation of the Winner*' which dates from the Diocletian period (286–305 CE).

Popularly known as the 'Bikini Girls', they featured in a mosaic in the Villa Romana del Casale in Sicily, a large agricultural estate that was probably owned by a member of the Senate or, possibly, Emperor Maximian. Between 1950 and 1960, Gino Vinicio Gentili excavated the site and around 1959–60 he discovered the mosaic that depicted young women running, playing games with balls, throwing the discus and lifting weights, with the toga-clad winner holding a crown.

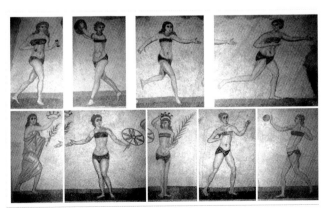

The famous 'Bikini Girls' of ancient Rome

A guide to Greek and Roman underwear

- Apodesmos – breast-band or girdle
- Indusium – an undertunic slip that hung from the waist, for matrons
- Mastodeton (also called mastodesmos) – a band that flattens the bust
- Strophium – breast-band belted over and underneath the breasts; soft linen, 6–8 inches wide and long enough to be wrapped twice around the body
- Subligaculum – shorts or loincloths worn by athletes of either sex (and actors)
- Subucula – a linen undertunic worn by both men and women
- Supparum – an undertunic made from linen and worn by girls
- Zone – worn around the waist and lower torso for shape and control

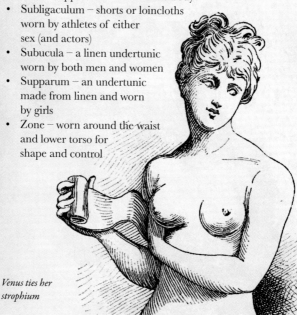

Venus ties her strophium

Similarly modern-looking undergarments also turned up in the ruins of the city of Pompeii, worn by a curvy marble statue of Venus. Leaning on Cupid, Venus removes her sandal, clad only in a gold-leaf bikini.

Lingerie in the Middle Ages

With the fall of the Western Roman Empire in 476 CE, the Church became dominant in people's lives, along with the fear of the raiding Huns and Goths and a new focus on basic survival. All roads no longer led to Rome and far-flung Roman trade was supplanted by local cottage industries, which meant that people had far less access to exotic fabrics such as silk; instead, the general populace now layered on tunics made of wool in muted hues.

It is unlikely that either sex wore anything that resembled supportive underwear, although both wore linen tunics, falling to the knees for men and the ankles for women. So few garments of any kind – outer or inner – have survived from the medieval period, that costume historians have gleaned much of their information from the Bayeux tapestry, which depicts over 600 people in a variety of clothing.

The Bayeux tapestry

Currently on display in Normandy, northern France, the tapestry is thought to have been commissioned in the 1070s by the half-brother of William the Conqueror, the Bishop Odo of Bayeux. It was handmade by Queen Matilda and her court to celebrate the Battle of Hastings in 1066. The 70-metre-long strip of linen is embroidered (despite being called a tapestry) with figures and inscriptions that show the Norman conquest of England.

From the dress worn by people in the tapestry, historians have concluded that apart from a linen undershirt, women in the Dark Ages probably wore no underwear.

Medieval masochism

The capture of Jerusalem in 1099 during the First Crusade seems to have been a turning point in the development of medieval dress. As people began to focus less on the afterworld and more on the present time, attention turned to concerns about what to wear. Returning Crusaders had brought with them the sartorial spoils of war, which included luxurious fabrics and new ways to cut and style garments. Women started wearing their long gowns fastened down the side, creating a much more body-conscious fit, which was snugly moulded to the torso by 1130.

The brocade fabric suggests inspiration from medieval times

The beginning of modern fashion

Costume historians consider the latter half of the 14th century to be the starting point of modern fashion. It was the period when the padded short jacket, known as the doublet, emerged. It was sometimes so short that it was considered scandalous. The surcoat, which was open at the

Garters are less popular today, due to the invention of elastic

The Order of the Garter

The chivalrous Order of the Garter, which originated in the Middle Ages, is today an exclusive club whose members include the British Royal Family and various foreign monarchs. It was said to have been founded by King Edward III (1312–77). Legend has it that the Countess of Salisbury was dancing near the king when her garter slipped off her leg. As courtiers snickered, Edward retrieved the garter and tied it to his leg, saying, 'Honi soit qui mal y pense,' (shamed be the person who thinks evil of it), which is still the motto of the Order today. When Edward ordered 150 garters for his knights, he had them made in Tartar blue, from what writers as diverse as Dante, Boccaccio and Chaucer all described as '*Panni Tartarici*' or 'Tartar satin', considered the world's finest fabric.

sides and stiffened in front, created the look of tight-lacing, described by one scholar as 'one of the most potent weapons of fashion through the ages'.

For women, the tops of their robes dipped ever lower and the décolletage emerged, showcasing high, pert breasts. This, combined with a fashionably curved belly and generous hips, was the ideal figure in the Middle Ages, related, naturally to a woman's ability to bear children. Women also began wearing proto-corsets, made of thick fabric, which had been stiffened with paste and laced at the sides. In general, it is not thought that these contained much, if any, whalebone and they were more for figure control than figure shaping.

A delight in display

Newly opened trade routes created an increasingly prosperous class of merchants with money to spend. They enjoyed spending it on fashion which developed rapidly – both in terms of the sheer adornment of the body and in employing a more tailored approach to putting it on display. The enthusiasm with which these early nouveaux riches enjoyed wearing their wealth angered the moral authorities of the day. An illuminated manuscript in the British Museum, dated from the end of the 11th century, shows what 19th century author William Barry Lord, author of *The Corset and*

The February scene from Les Très Riches Heures du Duc de Berry *(1410) depicts the worker's undergarments*

the Crinoline (1868) describes as a 'strange and anomalous' figure – a 'fiend of fashion' showing a demon in drag, dressed as a woman and laced into a corset, apparently as a warning against the growing excesses in fashion.

Later medieval underwear

Les Très Riches Heures du Duc de Berry is a book of hours, a devotional book containing religious content that was commissioned by the Duc de Berry around 1410. It is considered a key manuscript of the era. The month of February shows a worker sitting next to a fire. Skirts hiked up, she warms her legs. The illustration sheds useful light on the lingerie of the day, which typically included T-shaped and non-gusseted *bliauts* (tunics) that were belted under the bustline. Whether this was to accommodate frequent pregnancies or as a bust support is not known.

Court fashions

European fashions of the 16th century took their greatest inspiration from the courts of England, Spain and France and, in particular, the competition between Henry VIII of England and Francis I of France as to whose court was considered to be the most fabulous. When the

Holy Roman Emperor and king of Spain, Charles V, was succeeded by his son, Phillip II, in 1556, Philip's more sober tastes in fashion replaced the German love of 'bright colours and fantastic forms'. The new Spanish style favoured dark hues, preferably black, with a waist-highlighting, body-concious fit, which historians have noted reflected 'the stiff and proud etiquette of the Spanish Court'.

Padding for a perfect outline

Despite the sombre tones of their garments, the Spanish weren't too proud to pad their drawers, filling their doublets and hose with bombast so that wrinkles and folds were fully smoothed out. Men also began tight-lacing to make their waists look smaller and the introduction of knitting made it possible to create hose that were long enough to encase and showcase newly uncovered legs.

In addition, what had begun as a simple drawstring at the neck was now a high-standing ruff, which further emphasised the haughty high-class look, underscoring the fact that the wearer didn't have to work – or, possibly, eat. 'As the century progressed,' writes costume historian James Laver, 'ruffs grew larger and larger until it is difficult to see how their wearers could have conveyed food to their mouths.'

Catwalk fashion: with a tight fitting bodice and full skirt, this style may have taken inspiration from the 16th-century Spanish courts

A 16th-century stomacher, as worn by Queen Elizabeth I

The introduction of stays

With the spread of the Renaissance across Europe, fashionable courtiers favoured the rich silks and velvets from Italy and Spain that were now more widely available. These fabulous new fabrics were often interwoven with gold and silver thread and to show them off to best advantage, as well as support them (while sumptuous, they were heavy), they required a solid foundation. Silhouette-altering stays, as corsets were still called, buckram-stiffened stomachers, unbending wooden busks and crinolines all became prevalent at the end of the 15th century, along with the farthingale, a series of hoops worn beneath a woman's skirts.

The Spanish farthingale

Introduced to Britain in 1501 when the teenage Spanish princess Catherine of Aragon arrived to marry King Henry VII's son, the future Henry VIII, the farthingale had already been worn in her native Spain for several decades. It was rumoured to have originated with a 15th-century Portuguese princess who was attempting to cover up an unwanted, perhaps illegitimate, pregnancy. Earlier versions were worn on the outside of the skirt, like a hooped exoskeleton that had been stiffened, variously, with willow cuttings, rope, whalebone and giant reed – also

Henry VIII loved extravagant fashion and wore elaborately decorated codpieces

The age of the codpiece

In the film, *A Clockwork Orange*, the violence-loving thugs sport tone-on-tone codpieces. *In Do Androids Dream of Electric Sheep?*, Philip K. Dick's 1968 novel on which the movie *Blade Runner* was based, men protect themselves from becoming sterile – from the radioactive dust covering the Earth with nuclear fallout – by wearing lead codpieces. The male package-enhancing pouch, derived from the Middle English term 'cod' or scrotum, is associated with European men's fashions of the 15th and 16th centuries, when men's hemlines started to rise and despite longer and longer hose, their scandalously short doublets left them somewhat exposed. Henry VIII was thought to have kicked off the trend for ever more lavish codpieces; although known for his love of extravagant fashion, it was also possible that he used them to disguise the medicine-soaked bandages that helped to relieve the symptoms of syphilis.

known as 'green wood' or 'verdugo' and the origin of the word vertingale and later, farthingale. The Spanish farthingale later moved beneath the skirts, creating a bell shape that began modestly enough, but eventually grew to impressive proportions as the French farthingale.

The farthingale goes to extremes

During the Elizabethan period, a woman wearing a farthingale looked as if she was standing inside the centre of a wheel, with whalebone or wire spokes positioned at right angles to the waist that radiated outward in a platter shape. The remainder of the structure graduated down to the ankle, stiffened at regular intervals into an unwieldy skirt skeleton over which the outerskirt was draped, often measuring a distance that was wider than the wearer's outstretched arms.

Creating even more volume

The addition of the 'bumroll' contributed yet more volume. It was essentially an oblong fabric sausage stuffed with reeds that further padded the hip area and allowed skirts to drape with yet more panache. Wardrobe warrants from the period describe how dress pleats were further plumped

Queen Elizabeth I in an enormous French farthingale, a posthumous engraving by Crispin van de Passe, c.1603

A shopping list fit for a queen

Queen Elizabeth was known for her love of fashion – she bought gloves by the bushel and shoes in quantities that made the shoe wardrobe of Imelda Marcos appear modest. According to wardrobe warrants for her undergarments, they were crafted from a mix of leather, buckram, bents, and eventually whalebone.

The farthingale: a representation of fertility?

The reign of Henry VIII was dominated by his obsession with finding a wife who could give him a male heir, and so the course of English history was altered by his preoccupation with fertility. A woman's fecundity is traditionally determined, in part, by her 'child-bearing' hips, the very area of the body highlighted by the fashionable farthingales of the period. When Henry's daughter Elizabeth became queen, farthingales expanded ever further in width. Questions about whether she would marry and finally conceive an heir dominated her early reign. In speaking to 'all my husbands' (her people), she once remarked about how she saw her child-free legacy: 'in the end, this shall be for me sufficient, that a marble stone shall declare that a queen, having reigned such a time, lived and died a virgin'. While it is true that the cartoonish proportions of the farthingale could have been a display of majesty as opposed to femininity (costume historian James Laver compared the Elizabethan silhouette to that of a hobby horse), it all begs the question of whether the massive farthingale-supported silhouette allowed the Virgin Queen to replace her physical child-bearing hips with ones that were more metaphorical.

up with wadding, cotton and buckram. Walter Fyshe, who worked as Elizabeth I's tailor from 1557 to 1582, reported using the latter when he described 'making a Gowne of blak vellat with a trayne of the French fation garded with crymsen vellat enbrauderid with pearle lyned with crymsen sarceonett and buckram in the pleytes'. Not surprisingly, this extra layer of padding proved sufficiently unwieldy to be firmly out of fashion by the start of the 17th century. And while no extant examples of bumrolls remain, caricatures of the problems they caused to their wearers certainly do.

Whaleboned bodies

With the strong emphasis on the hips, the Renaissance silhouette from the waist up was less about being little in the middle and more about creating a flattened cylinder shape, with the roundness from the tops of the breast providing contrast against the board-stiff stomacher. The stomachers of the late 15th century were stiffened with glue, buckram, reeds and bents – with whalebones inserted directly into the lining of the outer bodice, in particular, down the front to the waist in a channel called the basque or busk.

Carved and engraved busks

Wider at the top than the bottom, the busk's close proximity to the breasts and heart caused it to acquire amorous overtones; examples were often carved with love poems, hearts, initials, dates and other tokens from men to their lady lovers that could be worn in secrecy. Whalers even gave them to their wives to remember them by while they were away on long sea voyages. To distract from the dangers of the job, they typically decorated the busks with happy, peaceful and love-related imagery.

The queen of extreme tight lacing

The change in focus from the flattened cylinder-torso to tight lacing that was designed explicitly to achieve a small waist can probably be attributed

Furniture for a farthingale

In order for women to be seated at least somewhat comfortably whilst wearing their farthingales, a special chair developed: a low, solid-backed stool with no arms and plain legs. The cushion and back were relatively fancy and typically upholstered in expensive foreign velvet, fancy embroidery, or 'Turkey' work – a knotted wool carpet with canvas backing and floral patterns that was produced domestically in the latter half of the 16th century.

to Catherine de' Medici. Although she controlled neither heart nor bed of her husband, Henry II of France (his much-older mistress Diane de Poitiers was reportedly so unthreatened, she even urged the king to sleep with Catherine to father more children), the Italian-born queen still set the tone of fashion.

The waist corset above alludes to the style of de' Medici tight lacing

A notorious iron corset said to have been worn in the time of Catherine de' Medici

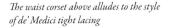

Catherine de' Medici prior to being widowed, painted by
François Clouet (c.1555)

Inconceivably narrow waists

In addition to the drawers, embroidered chemises and nightclothes she brought with her from Italy, Catherine de' Medici banned bulky waists at court; her ladies were encouraged to lace down to a waist circumference of 13 inches (33 cm) which, even by the petite body standards of the day is still tiny. 'French women have inconceivably narrow waists', confirmed a somewhat puzzled Venetian ambassador visiting France in 1577.

Catherine de' Medici introduced a formidable stay known as the 'corps' that made its wearers look 'imprisoned in a closely-fitting fortress'. Padded like armour, it was even thought to have functioned as protection by thwarting the assassinations-by-knife that were an ongoing problem at the time. The stays were hardened, stiffened and moulded from the

*An iron corset with a
13-inch (33cm) waist*

throat down to a long, unforgiving point. This was apparently a good thing, as this colourful quote from the late 1590s illustrates: 'I will have a petticoate of silk, not red but of the finest silk there is . . . it shall have a French bodie, not of whalebone, for that is not stiff enough, but of horne for that will hold it out, it shall come, to keepe in my belly . . . my lad, will have a Busk of whalebone, it shall be tyed with two silk points . . .'

A fun, although questionable, story about Catherine de' Medici is that she was so insistent that no wide waists be seen in her court that, once laced down to the appropriate size, a woman was supposed to wear an additional steel corset cover to keep her new waist size and dress fit exact.

A modern corset, courtesy of John Galliano by Dior

A corseted corpse

When the remains of Eleanora de' Medici were disinterred, her burial clothing, dating from the early 1560s, revealed two bodice layers, one made from velvet with 18 hook-and-eye pairs that connected up the front, over which was layered one in satin with a back-lacing. She was also found to have a more realistic, although still small waist size of 24 inches (61 cm).

Eleonora de' Medici

The corset-covers were made of thin steel plate, wrought into an open-work pattern, with drilled holes for a needle and thread to pass through when they were being covered in a luxurious velvet or silk. In order to open these metal corsets, they hinged lengthwise and were closed with a hasp and pin.

For correction, not fashion

While examples of iron corsets from the 16th and 17th centuries still exist, many scholars now believe they were solely used as orthopaedic or corrective devices. Their supposed role as torturous implements of fashion was undoubtedly a tall tale perpetuated by *La Vie Parisienne*. This racy, somewhat fetishistic turn-of-the-20th century magazine was probably also responsible for the Victorian myth of the chastity belt, for which no hard evidence actually exists.

When is a stay a corset?

The word 'corset' stems from the Old French 'cors' – a diminutive of the Latin corpus or body. It entered the English language in 1795 when *The Lady's Magazine* was attempting to differentiate between an informal front-lacing linen waistcoat that was quilted and unboned, referred to by the French as *un corset* and the typical heavy-duty stay. Stays were, in fact, how corsets were referred to until the beginning of the 19th century, leading scholars to argue whether it meant the female body was weak and in need of help, or something deeper and more sexually aware was in play. Rather than imprisoning the female form, was the corset actually a sartorial representation of the body and the lacing a stand-in for sex?

A typical mantua from the 1760s

The extravagant 18th-century mantua

During the reign of Louis XIV, France supplanted Spain as the leading European trendsetter. As the influence of the Sun King rose, the stiff Spanish silhouette of the previous century was replaced by the more loosely draped robe-like mantua, named either for Mantua, in Italy, where silk was produced, or from the French for coat, *le manteau*. The mantua was thought to better show-off clever dress design and highlight the expensive yardage of silk; although initially banned from court by

Robe à la polonaise had drapes which were pulled open to reveal the undergarments (1770)

the formal French monarch, it remained persistently popular until the mid-18th century.

The loose, robe-like gowns were worn over separate skirts and bodices, resulting in the first separate corsets, which were extremely long-waisted affairs designed to pull the shoulder blades together until they almost met, creating an exaggeratedly erect posture unique to the early 18th century.

The Enlightenment replaced many an ancient superstition with reason, sparking a newfound interest in mathematics. This fascination with geometric forms has been suggested as one possible explanation for the unwieldy mantua silhouette: an inverted triangular cone perched atop a rectangle and supported by a complex arrangement of panniers, stays and other elaborate underpinnings.

The extravagant robe *à la polonaise*

By the 1770s, fashion reached heights of elaborate adornment, creativity and fantasy, in particular with the popularity of the robe *à la polonaise*, which was pleated and pulled up in curtain-like swags to reveal the petticoats beneath. An odd homage to the country women of the day, the 'milkmaid' dress, as it was also known, mimicked the way in which

British pannier from the 1750s - these were mainly worn at court functions

the women pulled up their outer skirts to keep them from dragging in the dirt and, in doing so, revealed the underskirts.

The French radical thinker Jean-Jacques Rousseau was perhaps in part responsible, having started a trend amongst the fashion-conscious for everything 'natural' – including a movement away from excessive artifice in fashion. Cumbersome panniers which left the back of the skirt flat while pulling out the sides to widths of up to 1 meter (3 feet) were relegated mostly to court functions and heavy-duty stays started being replaced by quilted underbodices.

That being said, there were still any number of layers involved in being appropriately dressed, including a formal coiffure, stockings, appropriate footwear, petticoats and pockets – and all before being laced into your narrow-waisted stay.

Ode to la robe

Like any extreme in fashion, fun was to be had at the wearer's expense, as in this 18th-century poem:

'I cannot compare this new mode of the town, to nothing more like, tho' I know they will frown;
Than to a large hog-tub, that's turned upside down;
Large hoop'd petticoats, monstrous petticoats,
bouncing hoop'd petticoats, maids'.

An alternative silhouette

Like many stylish aristocratic women, Marie Antoinette had for some time spent her off-duty hours wearing the chic new chemise. This simpler dress was made from delicate fabric, belted with a sash and was soft and relaxed – just like the queen when she escaped to her private hideaway, Petit Trianon – a small château in the grounds of Versailles Palace where she entertained close friends and enjoyed some respite from the burdens of royalty.

When Elisabeth Vigée-Lebrun displayed a painting of Marie Antoinette in her chemise in 1783, it sparked something of a scandal as people accused the queen of having been painted in her underwear. The fact that the dress wasn't made from traditional French silks but from the new cotton muslin, a British colonial import, only added unpatriotic insult to injury.

Ironically, the Queen was probably depicted in her actual undergarments when Louis-August Brun painted the outdoorsy, sports-loving sovereign sitting astride a horse like a man. Trailing from beneath her short jacket is the long linen undershift typically worn by both sexes. Cut straight to just above the knee, the undershift would have had long sleeves and been worn next to the skin and under any corsetry.

Marie Antoinette, a leader of fashion

Despite being criticised for taking extreme liberties with historical fact, Sofia Coppola's film *Marie Antoinette* attempted to be faithful to the spirit of the woman and her love of fashion. Landing as a young, sheltered teen in a brutal foreign court already divided into factions and with no loyal supporters of her own, the young queen did attempt to take control of her own image. Historian Anne Hollander has pointed out that 'Marie Antoinette may well have felt her personal style was all she could manipulate'.

Actress Kristen Dunst as Marie Antoinette in the eponymous film, 2006

Regency corsets from 1819

Lingerie in
the 19th century

The French Revolution in 1789 signalled a huge political and social shift. Vast skirts, extreme corsetry and complex petticoats and panniers were thrown out with the ancien régime and simpler romantic fashions with high waists were soon adopted, which required minimal undergarments. But by the mid-1820s the waist had dropped again and stays, now known as corsets, were back in fashion, this time creating a more 'hourglass' shape to the figure. The 19th century saw a range of technological advances in the design of corsetry, including elastic lacing, as well as complicated contraptions, including crinolines and bustles, designed to support the skirts that were fashionable during the period.

Clothes go minimalist in this early 19th-century portrait of Madame Récamier, by François Gérard

Floaty, delicate dress t
distinctly 19th-centur

The impact of the French Revolution

Whether or not Marie Antoinette actually did exhort the starving peasants to 'eat cake', in her Rousseau-inspired white muslin gowns and sartorial homage to pastoral ideas, ironically she may have inspired the iconic 'anti-aristocratic' fashions of the post-revolutionary period. Following the French Revolution, women began un-corseting en masse, ditching the rigidly-moulded, overly-padded dresses and supporting corsets, camis, and underlayers. Instead, they chose softer, gentler layers inspired by classical Greece: floaty gowns made from delicate, draping

With a little help from below

The newly fashionable silhouette reflected the graceful, neoclassical columns of the period's architecture topped off by a capital or, in the case of the new dresses, the bust. 'The bosom, which Nature planted at the bottom of her chest, is pushed up by means of wadding and whalebone to a station so near her chin that in a very full nature that feature is sometimes lost between invading mounds', complained one observer of the day.

Linen and cotton gown from c.1800

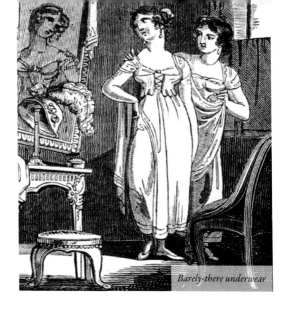

Barely-there underwear

muslin that highlighted a woman's natural shape. To create the look of being nude beneath, girls wore pink stockings and long, flesh-toned pantaloons styled on those already worn by men; they apparently even dampened their dresses for a more see-through look.

However, the new delicately draped muslin gowns were not unlike sheer nightgowns, meaning that most women required some assistance with both figure-shaping and modesty. Fuller-figured women, in particular, felt somewhat naked in the new mode and resorted to improvised corsets, bust bodices, and body bands to help create the fashionably rounded figure. Weather was also a factor. The filmy, flimsy fabric that was so well suited to the balmy Mediterranean, proved impractical and uncomfortable in the chilly damp of Europe. By 1810, women had once again started covering up, and the whalebone corset had reappeared by 1830.

Victorian vixens
Control regained – corsets and crinolines

The post-revolutionary period became somewhat renowned for apparently 'loose' behaviour which in later years was sometimes attributed to a lack of 'proper' undergarments Victorian women soon began layering them back on and in multiples. Being uncorseted was considered the mark of a prostitute. A certain moral discipline was thought to be reflected in the physical constraints of the corset. The virtuousness of a woman's nature could be ascertained by how tightly she laced her waist.

Unlike their 18th-century predecessors which flattened the breasts, the new 19th-century corsets came with cups for separation. However, by mid-century they had become so complicated to get into some that women kept them on for up to a week. The resulting hourglass figure was striking, as was the subsequent lack of bathing; outer clothing naturally needed to be protected from such dirty bodies, so women also wore a wide array of underlinens, including a chemise, drawers, petticoat and corset covers, as well as contraptions to provide the correct silhouette,

The Victorian art of getting dressed

- Drawers and chemise – a short-sleeved, later sleeveless calf-length shift
- Drawers – first made as two separate legs joined at the waistband and open in the crotch (bagginess kept the seam from gaping open)
- Combination – like a playsuit; starting in 1870s when outer silhouette was too tight for any extra under bulk
- Corset
- Petticoat – worn in multiples; if worn with a cage crinoline, then two petticoats were worn underneath and one over to soften the outline of the steel rings
- Underpetticoat
- Cage crinoline
- Skirt support – crinoline or bustle
- Corset cover
- Decorative petticoat
- Dress

such as the corset, bustle, crinoline, and various bust-improvers. In all, the typical Victorian woman wore an average of 11 pounds of underwear.

The striptease show

All the various layers and contraptions – not to mention the social norms and prudery of the era – kept the female form off limits. (Even corset covers were worn to hide the top of the corset from view.) Naturally, anything so forbidden automatically became irresistible, so it is not surprising that the Victorian period gave rise to the striptease show.

The first stripteases were simply women undressing layer by layer down to their chemises and getting into bed. The Victoria and Albert Museum has many objects in its collection, including embroidered stockings and bright pink corsets, which attest to a private aesthetic. Obviously, some underwear was meant to be seen, including the garters worn by can-can dancers and drawers with split gussets – guaranteeing that a high kick would deliver quite a titillating flash.

Innovation in production leads to new lingerie trends

Although the Victorian era is now synonymous with sexual repression, right down to the myth of piano legs being scandalous enough to require covering (while it is true that most furniture was draped with fabric and shawls, it was probably more to hide the fact that it was cheap), the era was also host of new innovations in lingerie. With the development of the sewing machine in the 1850s, undergarments that had been previously stitched by hand, could now be produced far more quickly in a greater array of designs and at cheaper prices, all of which boosted the popularity of underwear.

As the market for underwear grew, so did the circumference and elaborateness of the skirts they supported. The older horsehair crinolines or additional layers of petticoats that women had relied on previously just produced bulk and heft, where lightweight shape and structure were now desired. One enterprising inventor even filed a patent in May 1856 for an inflatable skirt, that could be deflated in order for the wearer to be seated. *Punch* magazine lampooned the idea immediately: 'Some idea may be formed of the labour which the present mode has rendered necessary, when we state that to fill the air-tubes of a single dress it takes the most expert lady's maid upwards of three hours and a quarter, even with the help of a good-sized pair of bellows.'

The cage crinoline

A few months later, the more practical cage crinoline appeared, made from spring steel hoops and cotton tape and promptly launched what *Punch* dubbed 'Crinolinemania', along with a host of other problems: modesty (when a woman fell down, the skirt didn't, revealing all), mobility (manoeuvering through narrow doorways and fitting into carriages) and accidents (knocking tea, china, or glass off shelves and tables; having tea and then catching on fire while clad in layers of highly flammable muslins and silks).

Modern day crinoline?

However, the new steel-spring crinoline was also much more lightweight and easy to move in. 'So perfect are the wave-like bands that a lady may ascend a steep stair, lean against a table, throw herself into an armchair, pass to her stall at the opera, and occupy a further seat in a carriage, without inconveniencing herself or others', wrote an approving *Lady's Newspaper* in 1863, further noting that the new crinolines did less to provoke 'the rude remarks of observers thus modifying in an important degree, all those peculiarities tending to destroy the modesty of Englishwomen; and lastly, it allows the dress to fall in graceful folds'.

The fashionable giant crinoline eventually shrank to a more discreet bell-shape that was flatter in front and curved at the back. As the bustle became *de rigeur*, styles of bustles themselves were as varied as the figures they enhanced. Some were made from steel while others were stuffed with horsehair and even straw, especially if a bouncy, cushion-shaped posterior were desired – according to a cheeky saying of the day – enough to balance a tea tray on.

The corset goes mass-market

A key part of the silhouette was the narrow waist, courtesy of the new corset which was now being mass-marketed for a variety of bust and hip measurements and body types – including slim, full, stout, and graceful.

(With brand names like the 'Swanbill' and 'La Fiancée', they apparently also promised results in the arena of marriage.) 'Corsets have become an indispensable accessory with the present fashions of tight-fitting costumes and waists lacing down the back or front. In spite of much having been said against their use, very few of the fair sex are without some kind of corset,' advised the *New York Times* in 1881 in an article on 'The Fashions for Summer'. 'A well-made corset, setting perfectly to the figure and not worn too tight, is one of the most necessary articles of dress.' Even young girls were corseted with 'a kind of broad belt . . . with shoulder pieces' starting as soon as they were in dresses; when a girl turned seven, whalebone stays were added to both sides, while from the age of 10 to 12, another bone was added in the back. 'Corsets for young ladies have busks, narrow whalebones, and very soft steel springs. Ladies' corsets of satin or other material have jointed busks, and are drawn in over the hips, making the front of the corsets very long.'

Queen Victoria's drawers

Few pieces of Victoria's underwear remain because it is thought to have been divided up and distributed amongst the Royal Household. There are one pair of split drawers and a buttoned chemise made from fine linen which the queen wore in the late 1800s. Both pieces are embroidered with the crown insignia, the initials 'VR', and a number, so they could be kept track of when sent to the laundry.

Corsets on the catwalk

The model-hiring practices of the 'fashion establishments' that marketed corsets presaged the way in which today's fashion industry uses ultra-thin models to sell the clothes. 'Once a week, she said that we could be allowed to take them off,' related one corset model in an article in the *Chicago Daily Tribune* in 1908. By making her wear increasingly snug corsets continuously for up to a week at a time, including during sleep, she was able to whittle the girl's waist down from 20 inches to a more acceptable 15 inches.

'At last the time came for us to take them off and what a relief that was. In a short time, however, they were put back on again and laced in smaller than ever . . . At last, though, I got so that the sixteen inch corset would lace up tight and I knew I was a successful model . . . Now I am proud of myself. Mistress has gotten me so that my waist is only fifteen inches ... Everybody admires my little waist . . . I am not sorry that I am a model as after all I have gone through I am well looked after by my mistress, and if she were to ask me to put on smaller corsets, I would do so.'

Exercise and a changing attitude to the female form

Corsets eventually fell from favour, reflecting sweeping changes in society. A number of women's rights activists, including Elizabeth Cady Stanton and Amelia Bloomer, advocated ways other than home, hearth and fashion that women could express themselves – including freedom of movement.

'The costume of women should be suited to her wants and necessities', wrote Bloomer. 'It should conduce at once to her health, comfort, and usefulness; and, while it should not fail also to conduce to her personal adornment, it should make that end of secondary importance.'

A costume specially designed for riding a bicycle

The bicycle boom and health corsets

During the era, the bicycle became extremely important to women, not just as one of the many 'health-giving' crazes that swept the late 19th century, but because it allowed them greater independence. Corset makers, sensing an opportunity, created a more lenient corset that was cut away at the hips and bust and less tightly laced to give greater movement and ease of breathing. The so-called 'health' corsets allowed women to begin to question the entire idea of wearing corsets, paving the way for their eventual abandonment. However, it is worth noting that perhaps they didn't disappear, rather they may have simply become 'internalised' with more modern ways of manipulating the female torso such as diet, exercise and, more recently, plastic surgery.

Tight-laced organs?

Although beloved by fashionistas, tight-lacing aroused the ire of many medical practitioners of the Victorian era, who blamed corsets to for a long list of ailments, including 'consumption, curvature of the spine, rib displacement, cancer, hysteria, hunchback, abortion, melancholy and epilepsy'. And while tight-lacing was equated with good moral standards, these same authorities criticised the fact that they appeared in erotic literature in order to titillate.

EFFECT
OF AN
OLD
STYLE
CORSET

THE
NEW
FIG-
URE

The 'S' bend corset

A particularly influential 'health' corset was introduced just before the death of Queen Victoria in 1901 by a corsetière with a background in medicine and a book to her credit. The industrious Madame Inez Gaches-Sarraute, author of *Le Corset: Etude Physiologique et Pratique* (The Corset: A Physiological and Practical Study), also had a desire to release women from corsets that she deemed detrimental to their health. The inward curve of the popular spoon busk was thought to suppress the bust and force the organs downward, which Madame Gaches-Sarraute solved by designing a corset with a straight and inflexible busk to support, rather than distort, the abdomen; her corset also began just below the bustline in order to free up the breasts.

The 'S bend'

Women were immediately enamoured of the new corset especially when they realized that if they laced it far, *far* tighter than Madame recommended, they could cinch their waists down to ever smaller extremes. To accommodate the straight up-and-down inflexibility of the busk, the hips were thrust back and the bust up and out, creating the fashionable S-bend shape. While stylish, the price of being a Gibson Girl (the personification of female beauty during the late 19th-century) included extensive lower back pain, hyperextended knees, difficulty breathing and breasts in need of greater support.

*Swimwear in
the 1920s*

From the invention of the bra to the 1950s

The 1890s produced the earliest versions of the lingerie item that became an indispensable part of every women's wardrobe. Originating as a sort of split corset, the brassière was refined by a series of enterprising female designers until by the 1930s, mass production had made bras available to all. New stretch fabrics and the invention of cup sizes made the bra ever more comfortable and sophisticated and the bustline an increasingly prominent erogenous zone. The early history of the bra probably reached its apogee with gorgeous Sweater Girls such as Lana Turner who wore torpedo shaped bras to show off their assets to the full.

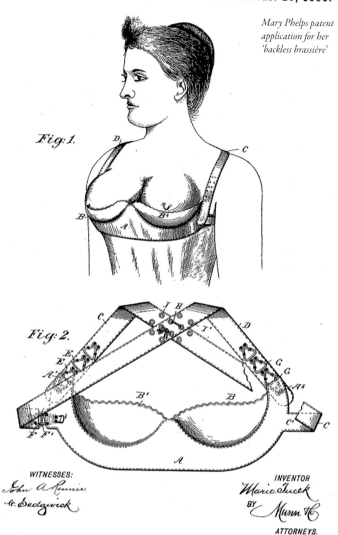

M. TUCEK.

BREAST SUPPORTER.

No. 494,397

Patented Mar. 28, 1893.

Mary Phelps patent application for her 'backless brassière'

Fig:1.

Fig:2.

WITNESSES:

John A. Rennie

C. Sedgwick

INVENTOR

Marie Tucek

BY

Munn & C

ATTORNEYS.

The invention of the bra
Marie Tucek and Polly Phelps Jacob

In 1893, a woman named Marie Tucek received a patent for what was described as a breast supporter. It was essentially an extremely low-cut balconette bra with straps that criss-crossed at the back and fastened with hooks and eyes, creating the low-slung bosom that was in vogue at the time. However, because Tucek never properly marketed her invention, the credit for its invention tends to go to Mary 'Polly' Phelps Jacob, a 19-year-old party girl who purchased a floaty gown for her debut into New York society, only to discover that her whalebone corset created unsightly lumps under the sheer fabric.

The myth of Otto Titzling
and the invention of the brassière

According to urban legend, the bra was invented by a certain Otto Titzling who lost a lawsuit to Phillip de Brassière (as in 'fill up the brassière'). While fun, the story is pure fiction and was originated by Wallace Reyburn in his spoof *Bust Up: The Uplifting Tale of Otto Titzling and the Development of the Bra.*

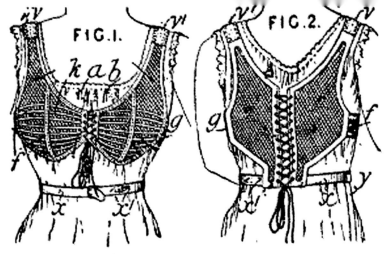

Diagrams showing the workings of Camille Cadolle's Le Bien-être

No more visible corset line

So she fashioned an ad hoc, corset-free solution: two silk handkerchiefs attached using cord and pink ribbon, and on 3 November, 1914, she received a patent for her 'backless brassière' and then launched the firm of Caresse Crosby. Better at working the social circuit than running her business, Crosby soon sold her patent to the Warner Brothers Corset company for $1500, and the company went on to earn millions of dollars from her invention over the following three decades.

Herminie Cadolle

And because designs are never conceived in a vacuum – as fashion historian Anne Hollander has observed: 'The collective imagination appears stronger than the individual one, and most designers work to serve it, not their own free inspiration.' French lingerie queen Herminie Cadolle was also responsible for some of the earliest bra designs. Clearly adept at PR, her glitzy clientele included royalty, famous performers, and even the spy, Mata Hari.

Cadolle further cemented her reputation as a bra innovator when she exhibited her new 'le Bien-être' (the well-being) at the Paris Exposition of 1900. Her two-piece waist corset and bust support with shoulder straps was soon separated and just the upper half marketed alone as a

Sarah Bernhardt's bra

The term 'brassière' seems to have first appeared in 1893 in the Syracuse Evening Herald which observed: 'Still of course the short-waisted gowns mean short-waisted corsets and those ladies who wish to be in the real absolute fashion are adopting for evening wear the six-inch straight boned band or brassière which the legendary French actress Sarah Bernhardt made a necessity with her directoire gowns'. But it wasn't until 1907 that the word appeared in Vogue magazine, and finally, in 1912, it made it into the *Oxford English Dictionary*.

Early bra designs, such as Le Bien-être provided the foundations of modern day bras

soutien-gorge. It proved so popular and widely imitated that the American patent office created a new category beyond just 'upper body coverings' and 'corsets': the 'brassière' (from the old French for 'arm protector' in military uniforms) for which Polly Phelps Jacob was the first to receive a patent in this new category.

The impact of the First World War and the 1920s

The First World War further conspired to kill off the corset in favour of the bra. As part of the war effort, women were asked to give up their corsets in order to free up steel – which they did – willingly providing more than 28,000-tons-worth, enough for two battleships. And while the old-school corset fell out of favour, the independent spirit of the Gibson Girl lived on in the fun-loving flappers of the post-war period who bobbed their hair, hiked up their hems and relished the flouting of convention.

Women's new reckless attitudes, mode of dress, and deliberately flattened bustlines raised eyebrows and questions. Though decried at the time as 'masculine' and 'boyish', on reflection they didn't seem so much masculine as childish; an air of 'girlish immaturity' clung to them, and dressed in shapeless rectangular-shaped frocks with busts bound to flatness, women resembled sexualised young girls, a theme that was to repeat itself four decades later in the 1960s.

To achieve the required no-bust look of the 1920s, well-endowed women laced up in the Symington Side lacer, while their small-breasted sisters had an easier time of it, typically opting for a simple bandeau bra, either store-bought or homemade.

The development of cup sizes

Although flat chests were all the rage throughout the 1920s, some thought the silhouette less than becoming. Ida Rosenthal, who ran Enid Frock on New York City's West 57th Street with her husband William Rosenthal and their business partner Enid Bissett, realised that a natural-looking bust was a more flattering shape for clothing. So in 1928, they added cups and elastic to the bandeau – separating the breasts and sizing them from A through D, creating the basis of the system that is still in use today. They differentiated their creation from the 'boyish' form of the day with the ultra-feminine name 'Maidenform'. During the 1930s, at about the same time college girls shortened the word brassière to bra, the Rosenthals changed the name of their company to the Maidenform Brassière Company.

Bra timeline

1893 Term 'brassière' used in the English language
1904 Manufacturers begin using the term 'brassière'
1907 Makes its inaugural appearance in *Vogue* magazine
1911 The term is found in the *Oxford English Dictionary*
1914 First patent is issued in the newly created category of brassière
1928 Modern system of bra-sizing with cups invented
1930s Name popularly shortened from brassière to 'bra'
1960s Decried by feminist writer Germaine Greer as 'ludicrous' and symbolically burned

*A long-leg lace
girdle by Wolford*

The development of the girdle

To achieve the boyish flapper silhouette, many a fashionable woman
(and a surprising number of modish men) resorted to gimmicky rubber
undergarments which promised to sweat away 'superfluous flesh' and
deliver a svelte silhouette. Designer Paul Poiret was one of the first to
be credited with using rubber to create a modern girdle designed to help
shrink and smooth the way for his hip- and booty-conscious designs. It is
thought that the designer originally made a rubber girdle for the ballroom
dancer Irene Castle, to help make the woman who was the toast of 1920s
Paris café society, more *soignée* on the dance floor.

Body sculpting underwear; an evolution of the rubber girdle

The development of Lastex

The Charneaux rubber-reducing girdle was particularly popular, by merit of its lack of restrictive boning but apparent hardcore ability to shape – and breathe. Being encased in a what was essentially tight rubber sausage casing was without doubt uncomfortably sweaty – and most ads for rubber girdles trumpeted their methods of ventilation: perforations that let in some air. By the 1930s, Dunlop Rubber company had developed a modified form of rubber with a two-way stretch derived from latex and marketed under the name Lastex, which led to the development of the modern panty girdle. Well into the 1960s, the girdle was still considered a must-have foundation garment for any well-dressed woman.

Why girdle?

According the website GirdleZone.org, which describes itself as a 'scholarly exploration of the social and erotic significance of a controversial garment', the girdle can help a woman keep it together mentally as well as physically: 'The held-in, held-together feeling produced by a girdle makes many women feel more organised, more alert, and more authoritative, as well as more attractive. Many women find that girdles make them feel more feminine, and more graceful. A woman wearing a girdle will walk and sit with a charming, careful grace that is distinct from the impressions produced by ungirdled informality.'

Weird and wacky moments in bra history

- In 1991 a woman died when the underwire in her bra was struck by lightning.
- According to the *Guinness Book of World Records*, the largest bust is a 48V, with a combined weight of 56 pounds (25.5 kg). Women's breasts can vary in weight from 10 ounces (285 g) to 20 pounds (9.1 kg).
- Triumph International invented a bra which released a fragrance designed to quench the desire for a cigarette.
- A bra was designed to detect radiation in case of nuclear attack.
- Eight out of every 10 women wear the wrong size bra.

Swimwear fashion in the 1940s

The parallel history of swimwear

Until the 1940s, women's underwear was primarily designed for body shaping. The firm Frederick's of Hollywood gets the lion's share of credit for creating a market in undergarments that were based not on function, or even comfort – but on brazen sex appeal. Instead of sturdy, plain-hued linens, women's lingerie started being sold in silks, satins, and lace, and in bright colours designed to appeal to men. The panty, in particular, surpassed its humble origins (hygiene) and the original granny pant was, in its day, regarded as extremely sexy. However, with all due respect to Frederick's clever marketing initiatives, the panty actually rose to sex symbol status courtesy of its close cousin: swimwear.

Swimwear design – ahead of the game

From the beginning of the 20th century, swimwear consistently developed ahead of intimate apparel, inspiring and pushing the boundaries of underwear design. One reason is that performance fabrics, in particular, Lastex DuPont's development of nylon (1938), and Spandex (1962), which they marketed as Lycra, all lent themselves well to intimate apparel. The other reason is related to the location where swimwear is typically worn: the seaside.

The beach is a place of 'pure' nature which has always existed outside the prevailing social and sartorial dictates of the day. Unlike the promenade that leads back to town (civilisation), the beach is simultaneously a reminder of nature's unruliness and its glamour. Located outside of the normal boundaries and expectations, the sea is a special, unique place, where different rules apply; as a result, people have always acted and dressed differently than in 'real' life.

Different rules at sea

During the early years of overseas travel, men and women mingled freely at sea. On the glamorous ocean liners that piloted the rich and fabulous to their international playgrounds, the social codes were far less rigid. According to *The Complete Book of Etiquette* by Hallie Erminie Rives (1926), 'formal introductions are really not necessary at sea' . . . The woman who dresses elaborately at sea . . . at once dubs herself a novice or a climber. So marked is the lack of showy dressing on shipboard that it is smart not to dress too smartly . . . any display of jewels is at once vulgar and dangerous'.

*swimwear fashion has come
ay from the knee-legnth one
the Victorian era*

From health cure to holiday pleasure

The original vogue for swimwear began with the Victorians, who swam less for fun than for the supposed curative powers of swimming which, in line with most Victorian activities, was done with a great deal of fuss and ceremony and included wearing elaborate skirted tunics, bloomers and black stockings.

As train travel became popular, city dwellers escaped the summer heat and headed to grand hotels centered around thermal springs thought to be health-giving for countless ailments, 'female troubles' included. The resorts eventually developed into 'self-contained universes of leisure' offering billiards, bowling, golf, tennis, horse riding and dancing to a live orchestra.

Annette Kellerman in her controversial swimsuit

Annette Kellerman

As more ways to travel developed, more people travelled towards the sun. And delicious scandals weren't far behind. Annette Kellerman, an Australian famed for her high-profile stunts involving swimming – attempting the English Channel, water ballet, high-diving – wore her fitted performance suit on the beach in Boston in 1907 and was arrested, even though her knee-length one-piece tank was almost identical to what men wore on the beach (with the addition of dark stockings).

For the next decade, men and women continued to wear similar knitted woollen costumes on the beach, but times were changing, and bathing costumes with it. As the spa hotels of the Victorian era were replaced by fashionable seaside resorts, one enterprising boutique owner in Deauville, in the south of France, made a fortune in 1913 from selling relaxed-chic belted jersey cardigans which she devised after giving up corsets – because they made it impossible to laugh.

Resort fashion

Always an innovator, Coco Chanel created the first fashions to come directly from a resort destination. When the wealthy American expatriates, Sara and Gerald Murphy 'discovered' the French Riviera in 1923 and spent the summer there, the beach resort had officially 'arrived'.

Getting married in cellophane

Jockey's cellophane wedding

Prior to 1934, the only underwear available to men were boxer shorts or union suits, one-piece full length knitted suits. Their options changed dramatically with the invention of the innovative, supportive Jockey brief. To promote their underwear, Cooper's, as Jockey was still known, staged a terrific publicity stunt at the 1938 National Association of Retail Clothiers and Furnishers convention. Because decency laws of the day would not allow live models to wear only underwear, the company cleverly turned to cellophane.

The models – dressed as a bride, groom and attendants at a mock wedding – were all garbed in transparent wedding garments, which showcased their underwear beneath. *Life* magazine picked up the story, as did Hitler's propagandist, Joseph Goebbels, who used it to demonstrate Nazi superiority by showing the new moral low to which America had sunk. Hitler waved a copy of the magazine in front of a frenzied crowd, decrying the immoral Americans who demonstrated their disregard for the sanctity of marriage by tying the knot without proper wedding attire.

Fashionable travellers wanted to reveal their suntanned bodies, which meant excess covering had to go, including the top of the tank for men, and increasingly skimpy suits for women. The late 1920s brought the *maillot de bain* or simply maillot, made from increasingly sophisticated fabrics that incorporated elasticity so that they did not go out of shape after swimming and were more comfortable to wear. And by 1932, Parisian couturier Jacques Helm caused waves (but hardly a scandal) when he showed a suit that exposed the midriff.

The bikini

And then, in 1946, the bikini made its splashy debut – and revealing a whole lot more skin became acceptable, eventually. Consisting of a bra paired with the loincloth-like bottom worn by wrestlers, it was considered so scandalous that no one would model it at first (an exotic dancer at the

Lord of the beach

The first bikini was printed with newspaper type, perhaps in anticipation of the flurry of press buzz its inventor, Louis Réard, anticipated it would generate (not to mention the 50,000 or so fan letters he received from men).

*Lingerie influenced
by the pin-up culture*

Casino de Paris had to be called in). The inventor was a French boutique owner called Louis Réard, a former engineer who was competing with Helm to market the smallest bathing suit ever.

Where Helm created the Atome, Réard responded within days of the high-profile first nuclear tests on the Bikini atoll with his two-piece of the same name; while the one-piece 'Atome' was widely advertised as the 'smallest bathing suit in the world', it was said that the bikini 'split the atome'.

Lingerie goes pin-up and progressive

Sexy lingerie in mainstream culture received a major boost during the Second World War, thanks to the pin-up culture. Although the noses of military planes had been decorated during the First World War, it was during the second that pin-up art – and, in particular, plane nose art – flourished. The main sources of inspiration were typically copies of *Esquire* magazine's calendar girls drawn by Alberto Vargas; popular comic strips, especially Andy Capp's Li'l Abner and anything by Milt Caniff; Hollywood, in particular Rita Hayworth as Flamin' Mamie, and, surprisingly, Disney.

Disney's studios in Burbank were located near the main Lockheed plants, resulting in an ongoing artistic collaboration. Fresh from the assembly line, the planes were decorated by Disney studio artists in decidedly non-Disney ways. Not only were racial slurs and derogatory commentary not off-limits, but the Disney art focused on portraying enemy leaders as negatively as possible, and had much nastier undertones than the relatively innocent and bouncy pin-ups drawn by the soldiers.

Pin-up art

When the cat's away

Pin-up nose art varied widely from tame to explicit. The further away from HQ an aircraft was based, the more likely it was to be adorned with nudity. Overall, though, pin-up nose art portrayed a free-spirited, daring woman who, unfortunately, became much more buttoned-up and domesticated after the war.

Glamor to boost morale

Although pin-up nose art wasn't officially sanctioned by the military, the men were not discouraged from sexing up the B-17 bombers (known as Flying Fortresses) with lovely ladies. 'Its purpose was worthy, to bolster military morale in a terrible time,' remembers Anne Josephine Hayward, herself a female nose art painter in England. 'The members of each crew came to feel that their plane and their painting were somehow special and would bring them luck, a safe return from hostile skies. The art may have been frivolous at times, but it was never anti-social.' The positive attitude reflected in the flying pin-up art was seen in the way the women were portrayed, voluptuous hour-glass babes that were, at the same time wholesome, and fit to be introduced to your mother.

Pin-ups and the changing role of women

No one was more lusted after, perhaps, than Betty Grable, who not only helped launch a new, more hard-edged style of post-war photography, but gave notice that a revolution was underway – a sexual revolution. Classic pin-ups also reflected the changing workplace demographic with millions of young women now working outside the home. For example, in the US between 1940 and 1944, so many men were away at war that the proportion of jobs considered 'acceptable' for women had risen from 30% to almost 85%, and the number of women following in the footsteps of Rosie the Riveter (a female icon in the US, representing the women working in wartime factories) rose to 20 million, reflecting an increase of almost 60% in the number of women working. Women not only proved they could do a 'man's job', but that they could excel at it, and enjoy the accompanying freedoms – economic and otherwise.

Working girls as pin-ups

The lingerie-clad pin-up art reflected this social change. Whether ironing a skirt for work or getting dressed for the day ahead, the most coveted and collectable examples of pin-up art typically depict busy 'working' girls. The lingerie in these pin-ups usually includes high-waisted tap pants that

Appropriate attire

During the war, female Lockheed workers were informed that in the interests of 'good taste, anatomical support, and morale', the dress code included, and required, both bras and girdles.

The Pirelli calendar

The most famous girlie calendar has never been available for sale. Beginning in 1964, the tyre company Pirelli began publishing this exclusive piece of eye candy as a way to gift important customers and celebrities. Discontinued in response to the oil shock in 1974, it was brought back once again in 1984. Displaying glamour photography at its best, over the years a bevy of A-list beauties have posed for the calendar's artful nudes, including Naomi Cambell, Gisele Bündchen, Kate Moss, Cindy Crawford, Penélope Cruz, and Heidi Klum.

covered their garter belts worn with a matching embroidered or floral bra made from fabrics like satin, silk, and lace. Although idealised, they nonetheless reflected the undercurrent of social change, as men – the primary consumers of pin-up – balanced this new role of economically independent women against their classic roles as variously, mother, housewife and sex object.

New notions of womanhood

The main consumers of pin-up art were the young, inexperienced boys who had left to fight in the war. When their tours of duty ended, the returned home with new 'continental' notions about what was sexy in – and on – a woman. From 1944 to 1945 Paris was considered the 'Brothel of Europe' following its liberation from the Nazis. With so many soldiers on leave patronizing whorehouses, an entirely new 'culture of prostitution' emerged, complete with its own set of customs and even language. Like soldiers everywhere, the Allied forces made sure that they were as well-acquainted with the feminine charms in as much of the European zone as possible, as this extract from *YANK* magazine, the army weekly from the Second World War reflects:

'The GIs will return from the far corners of the world with a cosmopolitan outlook – deepened, mellowed by experience in foreign lands. No man will ever be quite the same . . . The broadening influences can be seen in

Nice outfit ~ but can she sing?

The music industry helped cement the image of lingerie in pop culture. When the long-play record, the LP, was introduced in 1948, a new form of marketing was born: album cover art. Like pin-up cheesecake, the images had the same objective: to pull the potential buyer in. While the music aficionado would respond to the additional listening time a LP offered, the cover was designed to appeal to more 'primordial impulses', hopefully to turn a browser into a buyer. Singers like Julie London were considered both sexy and talented, but typically, the content of the album and its sexy cover were tenuously related at best.

any chance encounter between a couple of world-weary GIs'.

'Yeah, I was in the South Pacific a year', the sergeant says over a bottle of coke in the Columbia Club. 'It was hot, and it rained like hell. Boy, what mud!'

'Just like Ireland', the corporal says, 'except it was cold and muddy and rained like hell. How was the liquor down there?'

'Lousy'.

'So was ours. The dolls was mostly red-heads in Ireland. Some pretty cute tricks'.

'Was you ever in Big-Bosomed Bertha's joint in Oran?'

'Yeah. The liquor was terrible. Some pretty cute dolls. I was in Sicily, too'.

'Me, too. It rained like hell. And, mud! But some pretty cute dolls'.

'I picked up a nice little dish in a joint in Catania. It was called Scarface

Al Capone's joint by the GIs'.

'Yeah. His liquor was lousy. Then I went to Italy. It rained like hell, and mud eight inches deep. But the dolls was cute. Was you ever in Baldy's joint in Naples?'

'Yeah. His liquor was lousy. When you going to Normandy?'

'Pretty soon, I hope. I'd like to see that country. The dolls are cute, they say. But it rains like hell and the mud's terrible'.

'And they say the liquor's lousy. But anywhere to get out of England'.

'You said it, Mac. It rains like hell here, and the mud's awful'.

'And what they do to their liquor shouldn't be done to a dog. I'll sure be glad to get back home'.

'Me, too. But I sure hope it don't rain like it did the day we left Camp Shanks. Boy, was the mud awful!'

'And I suppose if there's any liquor at all left there it sure as hell will be lousy'.

'But there's no cuter dolls, pal'.

'Nope, there's no cuter dolls'.

Lift, separate and titillate: meet the Sweater Girl

When the soldiers returned home, it was perhaps only natural that they would compare the women waiting for them at home with the wartime competition and want the same level of sexiness and boudoir

Jayne Mansfield

chic. It was time for the entry of the Sweater Girl, a media creation who simultaneously showed women how to be sexy in the new post-war way, while at the same time luring them away from the workplace and back into the home full-time.

The return of domesticity

Now that women were working in far greater numbers outside the home – as many as during Second World War, and many of them married – a backlash was brewing. Male politicians, businessmen, newspaper editors and film scriptwriters encouraged the view that married women should not be at work. Women had been told since birth that their purpose in life was to get married and produce children, leaving the world of 'real' work to the men. Competing with a man for a job was especially frowned upon. Dr. Benjamin Spock, the author of *Baby and Child Care* (1946), the post-war child-rearing bible for an entire generation of new mothers commented, 'I think that when women are encouraged to be competitive too many of them become disagreeable.'

Everyone's a sweater girl

While by-our-standards curvy, models, some even of a 'certain' age, pretend to enjoy a coffee klatsch in their comely sweaters, the male voiceover intones: 'The sweater has come of age. It's now stylish with a capital 'S'. And today, girls from teenagers to grandmas have become Sweater Girls. Seems everyone is wearing 'em . . . Remember, girls, when you wore a sweater just to keep warm? Remember the Sloppy Joe and the ones designed more for whistles than for warmth? Well that's passé, the experts say. Today's sweater is right in the fashion swing'.

Lingerie for the good girl gone bad

In the opening scene of Alfred Hitchcock's movie *Psycho*, Janet Leigh's character Marion Crane wears a white bra and lingerie to underscore her 'angelic' side. After she decides to abscond with the money, Hitchcock referenced her dark deed by showing her changing into a black bra.

Staying at home

The stereotype of the stay-at-home wife was also reinforced through television, in part because so many people now owned a set. In the ten-year period between 1950 and 1960, the number of US homes, with televisions rose from under 10 per cent to 90 per cent. The popular TV shows of the day showcased women who were good mothers, expert homemakers and knew that father knew best.

Propaganda was relentless in driving home the message that the woman who married and stayed at home was a 'success'. The public wanted stability and cookie-cutter conformity, so when TV delivered shows about women, it was with productions such as Lucille Ball's *I Love Lucy*, built on the idea of a damsel-in-distress who needed a knight (her husband) to save her. The shows of the 1960s further sidelined women to the home and especially the kitchen, mostly to worry about and look after menfolk. The husband who made enough financially to support – and rescue – his wife enjoyed prestige and accolades.

The torpedo bra

To promote the new 'ideal' woman as sexier than her career-minded sister, sexually provocative and busty actresses such as Lana Turner and Jane Russell lifted, separated, and influenced an entire generation of men,

The Merry Widow

The 'Merry Widow' was produced to coincide with the 1952 film of the same name, starring Lana Turner. The original 'Merry Widow' foundation piece worn by Turner was a full-length, nylon voile-lined corselette, made with panels of black and white lace, and elastic yarn net. Getting it on and off meant dealing with a battery of hooks and eyes, and finally, a heavy duty zip.

Bettie Page in the jungle

young boys, not to mention future bra designs. Typically clad in a tight sweater, they inadvertently created the demand for the must-have bra: the military-influenced 'bullet' bra which debuted in the late 1940s, promising a girl 'maximum projection'.

When Maidenform introduced their 'Chansonette' torpedo bra, it became the most successful bra of the 1950s, selling almost 90 million units in its lifetime between 1949 and 1979. The new rigid social structure was reflected in the typical undergarments of the period: a hardcore, longline girdle that produced a elegant wasp waist, the pointy channel-stitched bra (perfect under the structured boned bodices of the day) and, for full skirts, the voluminous and swishy net petticoat. Of course, no 'proper' lady left the house without stockings.

Bettie Page – the erotic antidote

Not surprisingly, the erotic antidote to so much uptightness was a freewheeling, voluptuous 'jungle girl' cavorting in a skimpy leopard bodysuit. Bettie Page, the era's raven-tressed and extremely voluptuous Queen of Pinups, was typically photographed in saucy S&M play, either as a dominatrix or trussed-up as the victim. Either way, she – and her naughty nothings – provided a vivid alternative to the sugar-coated, squeaky clean good girls and housewives of the era.

Not your childhood bunny

In her tight corset, the Playboy Bunny reflected the shape and sexiness of Marilyn Monroe, but her bunny ears alluded perhaps to Disney or, even, Alice in Wonderland's White Rabbit – both figures from childhood play. As the sexual revolution changed society's attitudes towards the female body, the tension between the infantile and the sexual – a foot in the past but with a view to the future – proved both uncomfortable and fascinating.

Grace Jones as Vamp

Lingerie from the 1960s to the present

While in the 1950s no self-respecting woman would have been seen without a firmly-supportive bra – possibly long-line – and a girdle to control and flatten her tummy, the 1960s saw a radical shift in attitudes to underwear. The shape of fashion became more childlike with tiny, flat-chested models such as Twiggy, while the emergence of the feminist movement meant that many women were no longer prepared to constrain themselves in the name of fashion. Later, while advances in design and fabric technology led to a new range of comfortable shapewear, other women chose diet and aerobic exercise to tone and firm their bodies, making control garments partly redundant.

Screen shot from Elia Kazan's
1956 film Baby Doll

The 1960s youthquake

Although British *Vogue* had begun catering to 'youth fashion' amongst the
17 to 25-year-old age group as far back as 1951, the idea of young women
as an entirely separate market that started after the war didn't really reach
full expression until the 1960s when it coincided with another giant

trend: the baby boomers coming of age en masse. Teen purchasing power and social influence had never been higher.

The result was an extreme focus on youth that – as is typical with fashion's constant pushing of the boundaries of taste and propriety – resulted in the almost 'infant-chic' of the 1960s with icons such the baby-faced (and bodied) Twiggy and the popularity of items such as the babydoll negligee. Named after Elia Kazan's 1956 movie *Baby Doll* about a thumbsucking child-woman bride, it presaged the extreme youth culture of the decade ahead – as did Sue Lyon's Lolita and stars like Brigitte Bardot. The babydoll was most recently resurrected by a number of 1990s grunge performers, including Courtney Love who used it to great effect as part of a signature 'Kinderwhore' (literally child-whore) look.

New developments in lingerie

Although the 1960s are often associated with attacks on lingerie from feminists ('bras are ludicrous!'), the simplest shift dresses in shapeless rectangles (which meant there was no need for shapewear) and free love (no underwear), not all women were prepared to go about their business without some help underneath.

The babydoll

Since free love, in particular, had rendered the military overtones of the torpedo bra passé, many women sought a bra that created a more 'natural' shape. They also still wore full and half slips, in increasingly shorter lengths to accommodate rising hemlines, the babydoll, and ironically, given the youthquake shaking up society, the granny panty.

A new fashion spirit

As millions of baby boomers entered their teenage years, the staid mores of the 1950s were replaced and aged downwards, from sex appeal, to the average age of marriage (which became much earlier than before), to fashion and style. The quintessential 1960s rectangular dress silhouette was originally introduced by Hubert Givenchy in 1957 as the 'sack' dress, finessed by André Courrèges with an ultra-modern space-age vibe, and immortalised by Mary Quant as the decade's iconic mini.

In interviews, Quant has talked about how her invention represented a way for her and her generation to separate from that of her mother, by replacing 1950s formality with clothes that were more practical (allowing a girl to sprint after a bus if need be) – and representing a new freedom of movement, both physically and figuratively. While art students with money were the first to embrace Quant's creation and its 'muted sludgy organic' hues which referenced the Arts and Crafts Movement, the growing teen market (the baby boom didn't end until 1964) was quick to follow in their miniskirted footsteps, copying Marianne Faithfull's no-bra look and, in particular, the doll-like vibe of Twiggy.

The impact of Twiggy

A slight 90 pound (six and a half stone/41 kg), 5'6" waif with a flat chest and boyish haircut, Twiggy defied traditional notions of beauty and sex appeal. With her shorn locks, giant anime-like doll eyes and micro-minis, her image dominated the latter half of the 1960s, taking the extreme youthfulness of the decade to a new, almost infantile extreme. Terms like 'chick' and 'dolly bird' were coined to describe just such non-sexual looking women clad in provocative clothing.

Unlike the elegant, but more mature looking models of the 1950s – Barbara Goalan, Suzy Parker, Bronwen Pugh – Twiggy, in her girlish shoes, white tights and minis, seem to represent a pre-adolescent non-sexuality upon which people could project their collective anxieties about sexual freedom and social equality for women. Juxtaposed against her ultra-short skirts (at a certain point, hemlines rose to a point at which they simply couldn't go higher), her minimal bust and child-like face created an odd tension and erotic distortion in the way women were being represented in the media.

The soft core 1970s

For many young women, the 1960s and early 1970s resembled the 1950s, simply with groovier fashions. While others took part in the

When bras attack

In the violent 1965 sci-fi film
The 10th Victim, huntress Ursula
Andress dispatches her intended
victim with a fabulous, but
deadly, spiky aluminum bra that
shoots bullets.

sexual revolution, the conservative values of their parents' generation still applied to many of the new generation. Tough and independent, crime-fighting women like Charlie's Angels and Wonder Woman still wore ridiculously sexy ensembles to save the world (at least Wonder Woman was able to accessorise her corset/bodysuit with fabulous indestructible cuff-bracelets), a constant reminder to women that it was only acceptable to save the day with heroics, provided they still behaved and dressed 'acceptably' – that is they appeared sexually attractive.

Some women rebelled, tossing off their restrictive undergarments, including bras, girdles, heels, make-up, lingerie, copies of *Playboy* and other 'instruments of male oppression.' All of which made for excellent newspaper copy, but a less than exciting chapter in the history of lingerie.

Wonder Woman reimagined for a new era

A fight for social justice and happiness

Along with their intimates, women actively shed social oppression. In the US, with mass protest against the Vietnam War, the resultant shootings of protesting students at Kent State University, the Watergate scandal, and the murder of Israeli athletes at the 1972 Munich Olympics and the energy crisis, society was in social upheaval. Authors, including John

Updike and Kurt Vonnegut examined the search for meaning in what seemed to be a spiritually bereft and materialistic society.

Along with the women's liberation movement, the counterculture and the push for gay rights, three developments helped to change attitudes towards everything from women's sexuality to their lingerie: the empirical research on human sexuality carried out by Masters and Johnson, artists and pornographers fighting for free speech and the influential writings of radical Freudian psychoanalyst Wilhelm Reich, who promoted the idea that one of the most important secrets to overall health and happiness was a healthy sex life.

The bra burnings that weren't

Women who joined the feminist or women's liberation movement of the 1960s and 1970s were notorious for burning their bras, making an increasingly nervous male establishment wonder what they might torch next. But in truth the bra-burnings never happened. This urban myth was inadvertently created by Lindsy Van Gelder, a young a reporter for the *New York Post* who was covering a feminist protest against the 1968 Miss America pageant. As women filled a 'Freedom Trash Can' with the various symbols of their oppression – girdles, heels, copies of *Playboy*, and yes, bras – Gelder compared them to Vietnam War protesters burning their draft cards. 'I shudder to think that will be my epitaph,' Gelder has been quoted as saying: 'She invented bra burning.'

Embracing the pleasure principle

The idea of sex as the key to happiness drove the development of soft porn and the way that women were represented sexually. Television continued to shed its family-friendly image, obsessing with women's sexuality (in everything from soap operas to popular drama and prime-time shows) and 'wallowing' in sex. Because so many households had televisions, it became the obvious forum for depicting and discussing the impact of the sexual revolution, and discerning the fallout.

Straights, gays, crossdressers, feminists, beatniks, and traditional types and all kept company on the television; when an offbeat character wrestled with sexual issues, it was as if the plot was about individual choice – not the fact that the sexual revolution was upending 'the heterosexual nuclear family, patriarchy or the capitalist system.'

Sexy vamps in lingerie

Vampire movies have always provided an entertaining walk on the dark side, pandering to our fears with great helpings of gore, sexual tension and sexy lingerie. The seductive females of Hammer Studios classics –

starring the suave Christopher Lee as Dracula – look innocent, but with an enticing reek of danger. Part of the secret of their Hammer glamour were the ubiquitous virginal white nighties and sheer black negligees (once immortal).

In the 1980s Catherine Deneuve and Susan Sarandon similarly glammed up the vampire myth in alluring black lingerie in the stylish 1983 movie *The Hunger*. The 'dripping with sex' sensibility and disco soundtrack added just the right sexy touch to their tortured lesbian vampire 'love' affair. The more recent *Lesbian Vampire Killers* (2009) was a more goofy take on the genre, but a fun and campy lingerie-lookfest nonetheless.

Drugs, money and sexy lingerie: the 1980s

Sex, money and extreme greed filled in for sex during the 1980s, melodramatically showcased in movies such as *Bonfire of the Vanities* (which features Melanie Griffith as a devious gold digger in pearl jewellery and lingerie), *Working Girl* (Melanie Griffith, again, but here with a 'head for business, and a bod for sin') and *Wall Street* (which represented the getting of money as being more exciting than sex). Copious amounts of cocaine and intensive aerobic exercise created a new breed of hardbodied female and the market for athletic wear influenced lingerie, just as swimwear had six decades before.

80s-style lingerie by Kriss Soonik

Underwear in the 1980s

Women gravitated towards satiny lace-trimmed pastels and jewel tones, camisoles with a bra built in – all the better for peeking sexily from under a power-suit jacket – white stockings with garters, see-through body suits (why hide that gym-built body?) and negligees. Nothing came between Brooke Shields and her Calvins, highlighting the new importance of designer labels in the lives of Wall Street types now extraordinarily flush with cash. Television stars such as Cybill Shepherd sexed up shows such as Moonlighting in teddies, camis, and tap pants, which now virtually replaced the slip.

Men in tights

Men were becoming equally picky about their undies by the 1980s, opting for more flair, including tapered boxer shorts, and Euro-style bikini cuts. When Michael J. Fox wore lilac Calvin Klein briefs in the movie *Back to the Future*, other men followed suit by choosing colour, taking cues from Jockey's new pitchman, Jim Palmer, and football star Howie Long's colourful Hanes briefs. Whether in prints, colours or skimpy cuts, men's intimates started becoming much more exciting.

Barbie's blonde ambition

Madonna's über-sexed image, various controversies and scuffles with the Catholic Church led Mattel to say a firm 'no thanks' to the notion of a Madonna Barbie. However, Barbie collectors can still celebrate Blonde Ambition with the Heidi Klum Barbie, Goldie Hawn Barbie and, of course, the original blonde bombshell. The Marilyn Monroe Blonde Ambition Barbie wears a red carpet-worth, glam gold gown inspired one created for her by costume designer William Travilla.

Lingerie movies of note include *Flashdance* (a wannabe ballet dancer who moonlights as an exotic dancer), *9½ Weeks* (erotic S&M plus striptease), and *Risky Business* (a dancing Tom Cruise in tight white underpants, and a sexy-as-hell, but lightfingered, hooker).

The Madonna effect

Ever since video killed the radio star in 1981 and music videos made a singer's look as important as their vocal talent, Madonna, in particular, has used lingerie to great effect in shaping her image. Her Lolita-like bustier and tulle skirt look in *Like a Virgin* (1984) helped spark the 1980s

Madonna, the queen of underwear as outerwear

innerwear as outerwear trend, while the Material Girl caused controversy in *Open Your Heart* (1986), which simulated a peep show in which she wore a *très* 50s black cone-bra bustier with gold-tipped nipples from which swung fabulous stripper tassles.

She later had French designer Jean Paul Gaultier – himself a longtime *enfant terrible* of the fashion world – design her iconic rocket-cone bra for her Blonde Ambition Tour of the early 1990s. Inspired by his grandmother's corset, the notorious bullet-busted bodysuit proved the ideal way to sum up a show that was denounced by the Vatican for its themes involving sexuality, cross-sexuality, and Catholicism, all while attempting to redefine the concert-going experience in a blend of style, fashion, performance art and the glamorous feel of a Broadway musical.

Open your mind

In her video *Open Your Heart*, Madonna sings about heartfelt love while performing a peep show number in a be-tasselled bustier. While many found her choices in the video morally questionable – from the male voyeurism to placing a little boy in such a seedy environment – others applaud the ending, where she exits the building wearing a man's suit, links arms with the boy while both leave dancing. 'Madonna is calling the shots for herself as she chooses innocence and purity over self-exploitation. The message to young girls was to own their sexuality for their own personal enjoyment, not for the sake of giving it over to Mr. Right.'

Debbie Harry

Lingerie in popular culture: film, music and dance

The power of film to translate a look into a worldwide trend dates back to the 1920s and 1930s and the development of the Hollywood machine and applies as much to lingerie as it does to outerwear. Film has also used lingerie to represent women as a wide range of archetypes, from virginal purity to raunchy sex goddess and from victim to predator. Female musicians and dancers have used the symbolism of lingerie to create a host of different stage personalities and also to make statements about society, culture and politics. The most recent, and one of the most powerful, exponents of this usage is the ubiquitous Lady Gaga.

Lingerie and the ultra-modern woman

The way in which Madonna, the ultimate Material Girl, not only embraced her sexuality but flaunted it to gain serious fame and wealth challenged feminist notions about what could – and should – be considered 'woman-friendly'. On the surface, Madonna's video images and the way she portrayed herself in her stage shows were overtly sexualised and seemed at odds with the ideals of feminism, but her control and manipulation of her image were anything but. Today, the singer and performance artist, Lady Gaga has reinforced the idea that flaunting your lingerie-clad bod is no longer a traditional 'sex sells' manoeuvre, rather many of today's women view it as a very 'my body, my choice' expression of their power. 'For today's 'power' woman, there is a strong female idea where wearing your underwear and expressing your power are not seen as contradictory', explains Sally Lohan, West Coast Content Director and Vintage Directory Editor for WGSN, a leading firm of fashion trendspotters. 'It is considered empowering and uplifting.'

In charge and out there

Educated, in charge and economically independent, these women see nothing demeaning in being extremely feminine and sexual as well.

The modern woman is not afraid to flaunt her sexuality and express her power through fashion

These same women are fans of modern burlesque, and stars like Dita Von Teese and Immodesty Blaize perform for audiences that are, on average, comprised of more than 70 per cent women. And more women are also watching porn – and admitting to it – while pop culture is saturated with titillating girl-on-girl action.

'Lesbianism is increasing since anxious, unmasculine men have little to offer,' adds cultural critic Camille Paglia. 'What I do on stage is to reinforce the notion of feminine allure and the glorification of women's sexuality and femininity,' confirms Immodesty Blaize.

The majority of the audience at burlesque shows are women

The notion of stripping as a celebration of womanliness actually has a surprisingly lengthy history. According to Camille Paglia, it is a 'sacred dance of pagan origins' with a long tradition in cultures in Egypt, Greece, Rome, India, Africa, and the Pacific Islands – in which 'the more a woman takes off her clothes, the more power she has.'

This theory suggests that women who attend burlesque (or Lady Gaga) shows are essentially paying homage to the 'pagan' goddess, while she, in return, is taking politically correct discourse about sex and returning it to a more interesting place. Naturally many women who have concentrated on their careers are less than thrilled to find that brainpower and hard work is so easily trumped by a young firm-bodied girl prancing around in her underwear, or, to quote Paglia: 'by a young hussy flashing a little tits and ass.'

Human progress is no longer considered to be a process of continual evolution, a single sweeping narrative dominated by science and rationality. Instead, history is now considered to be a patchwork of stories from a variety of cultures around the world. The result is a multicultural, magpie-like 'Age of Appropriation', which makes life more confusing, but at the same time richly kaleidoscopic and interesting. In this age, women like Madonna and Lady Gaga are simply reasserting their place – and perhaps vicariously, that of all women – on the erotic foodchain.

Elizabeth Taylor as
Maggie the Cat

Lingerie in the movies
Jane Russell in *The Outlaw*

One of the most influential sources of modern lingerie imagery is film. *The Outlaw*, which appeared in 1943, is probably little seen these days, but almost everyone will be instantly familiar with the movie's poster of Jane Russell. Languishing in the straw, pistol in hand and top cut extremely low to better display her superlative cleavage, the image propelled the film straight into the censors' snare and the actress to international sex symbol status. The movie's plot was also eclipsed by the story of a single piece of lingerie: the special bra with cantilevered underwire that the director, Howard Hughes, designed for the star to better display her ample assets (the actress refused to wear the uncomfortable garment).

Elizabeth Taylor as Maggie the Cat

The 1958 movie adaptation of Tennessee Williams' play *Cat on a Hot Tin Roof* is famous for showcasing a stunning Elizabeth Taylor in her prime, posed provocatively in white heels and a close-fitting white full slip as Maggie the Cat. Despite her obvious sex appeal, her drunken, ex-football player husband Brick (Paul Newman) refuses to sleep with her, believing that she was unfaithful with his best friend, Skipper, who recently committed suicide. In the toned-down movie version, Skipper's death was blamed on weakness; however, in the original version of the play, Brick and Skipper had been lovers and Maggie was simply trying to get rid of her rival. Cancer and in-fighting over the family fortune round out this juicy Southern tale of lust, lies and lingerie.

Pam Grier and 1970s 'blaxploitation'

She played a sadistic lesbian prison guard (*Women in Cages*); a sexy cellmate in a tropical prison (*Big Doll House*); a gorgeous thief chained to a fellow inmate in a South Seas prison (*Black Mama, White Mama*); a vigilante nurse and 'baddest one-chick hit squad that ever hit town!' (*Coffy*); and a revenge-seeking woman who looks sexy yet kicks serious ass (*Foxy Brown*). As the reigning queen of 1970s women-in-prison and blaxploitation films, Pam Grier was the original hot female action star and always looked outstanding posing for frequent movie stills and publicity shots in camply accessorised sexy lingerie.

Carrie Fisher and Princess Leia

An entire generation of Star Wars nerds fell for Carrie Fisher's Princess Leia at the beginning of *Return of the Jedi* (1983) when she was held

Carrie Fisher in her infamous gold sci-fi bikini

captive by the crime lord/blob Jabba the Hutt whilst wearing a brass bra, thong and sheer chiffon harem skirt. The ensemble earned Leia the number one spot on *Maxim* magazine's 'Hottest Nerd Crush' list.

'There's no doubt that the sight of Carrie Fisher in the gold sci-fi swimsuit was burned into the sweaty subconscious of a generation of fanboys hitting puberty in the spring of 1983', observed *Wired* magazine 'But, remarkably, it's women for whom the costume holds the most enduring meaning today'. The sexy slave costume has proved a popular choice for fans at conventions such as Comic-Con and Dragon Con, and made appearances on *Friends* (worn by Rachel to fulfil Ross's fantasy), *Family Guy*, *Robot Chicken* and even on *Dancing with the Stars* – when dancer

A slave to Princess Leia

Princess Leia's 'slave' costume was inspired by the work of fantasy artist Frank Frazetta, and required a mold of Carrie Fisher's torso to ensure that the fit was precise. The moldmaker chosen to do the body cast reputedly became so excited that he talked about it every day, causing the production department to become concerned, and, eventually, to give the job to someone else.

Kym Johnson wore it to tango with former 'N Sync member Joey Fatone, himself attired in a Jedi-inspired suit.

Susan Sarandon in *Pretty Baby*

Victorian lacy camisoles and bloomers never looked as sexy as they did on a sensual Susan Sarandon in Louis Malle's 1978 movie, *Pretty Baby*. Set in 1917, it was based on the photographs that local photographer Ernest J. Bellocq took of prostitutes in Storyville, the then-legal red light district of New Orleans. Unfortunately, the movie was overshadowed by controversy about the parts that dealt with child prostitution and a 12-year old Brooke Shields in the nude.

Two years before *Pretty Baby*, as part of her strategy to turn her into a star, Brooke Shields' mother had commissioned photographer Gary Gross to

shoot her daughter, then aged 10, in heavy makeup, her body heavily oiled and standing naked in a bath.

The 1975 image was later photographed by contemporary artist Richard Prince in 1983, and renamed Spiritual America. This image not only outraged the people who questioned the artistic authenticity of Prince's copy, but it also reignited the controversy over the content of the original work.

However, the furore that images of naked children create in modern society actually reveals a disturbing ignorance by the mainstream public of fine art and art history. 'After all, ban Brooke in her bathtub and the only logical progression is to censor the legions of pre-pubescent putti that populate every other classical painting. Where – and how – do we draw the line?'

Racquel Welch in *One Million Years BC*

'Travel back through time and space to the edge of man's beginnings … discover a savage world whose only law was lust!' promises the marketing tagline for this 1960s adventure/fantasy starring Raquel Welch. A Hammer Studios remake of an earlier film from 1940, it was, to a large extent, an excuse to show off the curvaceous star in her skimpy cavebabe fur bikini, fleeing various giant fauna and even dinosaurs despite the fact that they had become extinct approximately 64 million years earlier. (The movie's dinosaur animator, Ray Harryhausen, pointed out that he did not make the film for 'professors' who, he opined, 'probably don't go to see these kinds of movies anyway'.)

Not surprisingly, the publicity shot of Welch remains the film's most famous legacy. At the time, the studio 20th Century Fox sponsored a press junket to the Canary Islands where the exterior scenes were shot yet the world-famous shot of Welch was snapped by the unit still photographer, for which he never received more than his regular weekly paycheck.

The curvaceous Racquel Welch in One Million Years BC

The silky nightie retains its popularity on the modern-day catwalk

Fay Wray in *King Kong*

Beauty kills – in this case, a gigantic lovelorn ape named Kong, cornered atop New York's Empire State Building while clutching a beautiful blond in a silky nightie. A film about filmmakers shooting footage of Kong, this early example of post-modern deconstruction presaged the simultaneous fascination with violent and unpredictable nature and human attempts to convince themselves that they can control it. 'My dream is to save women from nature', Christian Dior once commented, while cultural critic Camille Paglia has noted that in our attempts to veer away from anything too overtly associated with nature's unruly side, we 'select, editorialise, and enhance ... Our idea of the pretty is a limited notion that cannot possibly apply to the earth's metamorphic underworld, a cataclysmic realm of chthonian violence. We choose not to see this violence on our daily strolls. Every time we say nature is beautiful, we are saying a prayer, fingering our worry beads'.

In the 1976 remake, King Kong removes Jessica Lange's bra

When it was premiered at the Radio City Music Hall in New York in 1933, *King Kong* enjoyed the most successful opening weekend ever to that point, grossing $90,000 – this at a time when movie tickets cost just 15 cents. Today, that would translate into more than $5.4 million gross.

The panties in *Sixteen Candles*

Sam Baker (Molly Ringwald) is turning 16 and in the excitement of her sister's wedding the next day, Sam's entire family has forgotten that it's actually her birthday. In this 1984 John Hughes' teen comedy, Sam's increasingly miserable day seemingly can't get any worse – until she finds

Hollywood's tallest, darkest leading man

'He told me he wanted me for a new adventure epic which would star the tallest, darkest leading man in Hollywood history', remembers actress Fay Wray about a meeting with producer Merian Cooper in 1932. 'I got excited and jumped and said "Clark Gable is coming over to RKO?" He shook his head and instead showed me a tiny ape, no more than 18 inches tall and Mr. Cooper said this was the mighty Kong and he was going to change movie history. I laughed nervously because I didn't know what I'd gotten myself in for.'

Kim Basinger

out that the geeky freshman with a crush on her has been charging $1 admission in the boy's bathroom to an impromptu peepshow – of a pair of her panties.

Kim Basinger in *9½ Weeks*

A movie about bad people enjoying good sex and juicy erotic sadomasochism, *9½ Weeks* (1986) includes a notorious scene in which Kim Basinger is blindfolded in the kitchen while a sexually dominant Mickey Rourke feeds her mystery foods. Ostensibly about the 'hostility, risk, and aggression' that fuels people's sexual lives, not to mention 'a frank depiction of the dynamics of sexual power', what really makes the movie worth watching is the fun striptease scene. Set to Joe Cocker singing 'You

Can Leave Your Hat On', a backlit Basinger playfully strips off her 1980s power suit to reveal a silky, thigh-length white slip over matching garters and stockings.

Showgirls

Remembered mostly for its stupid plot, terrible dialogue, bad acting – and a grievous mispronunciation of Versace as ver-SAYCE – the trashy lap-dance cult classic (1995) is actually a mid-90s commentary on the whoredom of fame. Essentially a retelling of the story of a good girl who goes to the big city to make it in showbusiness, sells part of her soul to become a star, and then repents, director Paul Verhoeven added a timely twist by making the ingénue less-than-innocent and more than a little crazy.

While the film was marketed as a sexy movie about strippers, what audiences saw – and reacted to so badly – was the 'exercise in subversive excess that makes violence sexy and sexuality violent, works overtime to make its non-stop T&A abhorrently non-erotic, and turns the traditional wide-eyed heroine into a frenzied sociopath in need of Thorazine'. And how better to visually represent such a scene than with skimpy showgirl costumes and cheesy lingerie?

Elizabeth Berkley
in Showgirls

Teen slasher movies

In many popular horror movies, in particular so called 'slasher flicks', the survivor is typically a teenage girl known as the 'final girl.' Less morally lax than her prettier, more sexually loose, party-hard pals, the final girl usually is the first to sense danger or realise that her peer group has perpetrated an injustice. As the various teens die at the hands – or knife/chainsaw/razored-glove – of the killer, the final girl starts to become more adept, more ballsy, more masculine, until, as sole survivor, she faces down her abject terror to dispatch the killer.

Interestingly, the audience for slasher movies is overwhelmingly male, and their motivation for watching may be driven by the fact that they believe some women 'deserve' what happens to them, while the final girl doesn't. The various beautiful girls who are dispatched by the killer are possibly a representation of all the various out-of-their league women who throughout the years turned down the male viewers, thus allowing them to enjoy their comeuppance: torture, rape, murder – or, perhaps, all three. When the final girl starts to fight back, she earns a respect which sets her apart from her more glamorous friends. And when she finally kills the killer, the male audience members actively support her and identify with her, assuaging any guilt they might have for vicariously indulging in and enjoying the raping and pillaging of the others.

Devanny Pinn

'I get rained on, thrown out of a car, hit by a truck and all in my underwear.'

Scream Queen Devanny Pinn on her role in the Christmas holiday zombie film *12/24*.

Zombie lingerie

The New Zealand label, Lonely Hearts created a collection of lingerie inspired by horror flicks *The Undead* and porn star Jenna Jameson's *Zombie Strippers*: 'Have you ever sucked face with a zombie chick?' asked the tagline for the Brains for Dinner collection.

Along the way, the audience gets to enjoy plenty of shots of beautiful young women in skimpy lingerie along with with their helpings of popcorn and carnage.

Marilyn Monroe in *The Seven Year Itch*

Few women have been as iconic, enduring, or influential in pop culture as Marilyn Monroe. Countless editorial and advertising photoshoots continue to reference Marilyn; sexy starlet Megan Fox has her likeness tattooed onto her forearm, and Madonna skyrocketed to mega-fame channelling while Marilyn. It's as if she is the sexy benchmark against which women continue to measure and compare their own sex appeal. Aside from Andy Warhol's Marilyn, the most iconic shot of the bombshell actress is the famous film still from the 1955 movie, *The Seven Year Itch* which shows Marilyn in a white halter dress, standing over a subway grate

The iconic shot of Marilyn standing over a New York subway grate

in New York with her skirt billowing up to reveal matching white panties. Although the movie was the smash hit of 1955, it has long since been eclipsed by the subway grate photo.

Whether it was the rowdiness of the crowd ruining the sound or the fact that Marilyn's white panties proved too sheer to pass muster with the censors of the day (she reputedly had to wear multiple pairs of underpants in an attempt to conceal her pubic hair; as shooting progressed, photos show her wearing longer and longer panties), the final image used to promote the movie revealed just the smallest glimpse of her panties, perhaps to help neutralise the overt sexuality of the shot. Of course it didn't. Marilyn's obvious exhibitionist tendencies combined with what

The foundation of fashion

The style of skirt on Marilyn's Monroe's Seven Year Itch white dress was introduced by Christian Dior in his post-war New Look, a sartorial reaction to the deprivation and fabric rationing of the war years. However, as Monsieur Dior once remarked, 'without a foundation, there can be no fashion' and his voluminous skirts in the Corolle line (some requiring up to 12 metres of fabric) were designed to be paired a range of specially designed sheer stockings that came in colours from delicate blush to bold black, to create an overall look 'at once elegant, feminine and provocative.'

The 23rd Street itch

Did the Marilyn subway grate shot have its inspiration in a far earlier shot? In 1901, Edwin S. Porter, a film director who worked for Edison's production company used a slow motion technique to capture the cheeky results of a skirt colliding with a subway grate. Shot in New York, the Edison Catalog billed *What Happened on 23rd Street* as 'a winner and sure to please.' On offer was a sneak-peek of when a 'young lady's skirts suddenly raised to an almost unreasonable height, greatly to her horror and much to the amusement of the newsboys, bootblacks, and passersby.'

Freud defined as our natural voyeurism (curiosity) about what's hidden under a sexy girl's skirts created a powerful brew that's still potent today.

Frank-N-Furter and *The Rocky Horror Show*

A certain 'sweet transvestite from Transsexual, Transylvania' made it clear that fun with lingerie should extend across genders and galaxies. The Rocky Horror Show, originating on the London stage in 1973 was brought to the screen as *The Rocky Horror Picture Show*. It featured bisexuality, homosexuality, sex with a manmade man, cannibalism, murder, and a fabulous finale: a cross-dressing

Tim Curry in
The Rock Horror
Picture Show

A sweet, long-running transvestite

Tim Curry's Frank-N-Furter still prances around in his
skivvies on the midnight-movie circuit as the star of the
longest running theatrical release in film history. On the
occasion of its 30th anniversary in 2005, the film was
selected for preservation by the United States Film Registry
of the Library of Congress for being 'culturally, historically,
or aesthetically significant.'

Busby Berkeley-style cabaret-style performance in full drag and in a swimming pool. As the characters swim and intertwine erotically, the protagonist, Dr. Frank-N-Furter sings 'Give yourself over to absolute pleasure. Swim the warm waters of sins of the flesh. Erotic nightmares beyond any measure. Don't dream it. Be it. Don't dream it. Be it . . .'

Partly a critique of the sexual excesses of the 1960s, partly the announcement of the dawning of new culture, Rocky Horror was an early summation of a number of maxims that are now common today: living materialistically for 15 minutes of fame, violence as a form of porn, and the idea that at a time when breaking taboos is so common, the most transgressive behaviour possible is in fact acting 'normal'.

The allure of the older woman

'Mrs. Robinson, you're trying to seduce me ... aren't you?' Dustin Hoffman's Benjamin suddenly – and awkwardly – realises in *The Graduate* (1967), as both he and the viewer become riveted by the sight of Mrs Robinson's garters peeking seductively out from under her dress. With a single stocking-clad leg, propped casually yet so provocatively on the barstool next to her, Anne Bancroft's Mrs Robinson put the world on notice that a new kind of sexual predator was on the prowl.

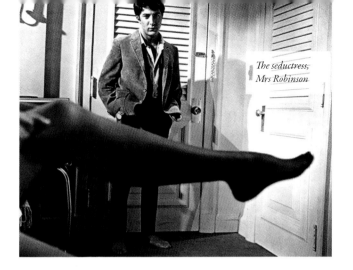

*The seductress,
Mrs Robinson*

And thanks to good jobs, the gym, a good diet, even better plastic surgeons, and a rising divorce rate, Mrs Robinson would be in good company today. Meet the cougar: hot, horny, over the age of 35, after fresh meat at least 10 years her junior, and armed with a bod that's still made for sin.

The rise of the 'cougar'

American primetime TV shows like *Cougar Town*, *Desperate Housewives* and *Grey's Anatomy* are filled with sexy, 'older' women in the mood for much-younger nookie, while Hollywood actresses including Demi Moore, Halle Berry, Mariah Carey and Eva Longoria have married much younger men.

Stifler's mom in American Pie

With Simon and Garfunkel singing Mrs. Robinson in the background, Stifler's mom made a giant leap forward in the name of the sexually attractive older woman . . . by hopping onto a pool table in *American Pie* (1999). As she drunkenly seduces one of her son's 'frenemies', a High School senior named Finch – first asking 'Mr. Finch, are you trying to seduce me?' – she insists as they're doing the deed that he call her 'Stifler's Mom'

A 43-year old mother of two, the former child star. Brooke Shield looked superb splashed across 28 pages of Australia's *Kurv* magazine, much of it in sexy lingerie showcasing her figure.

Well into her 30s, Demi Moore shimmied topless in the movie flop *Striptease*, and at 40 was voted 'Sexiest She-Villain' (Vilana más Sexy) at the MTV Movie Awards in Mexico in honour of her amazing bikini body in *Charlie's Angels: Full Throttle*. Cindy Crawford also recently graced the pages of *Allure* magazine in April 2009 at age 43 only moderately covered in soap suds.

Samantha Jones: TV's sexiest cougar?

Sex and the City's resident gorgeous older woman almost single-handedly managed to make the term 'cougar' a badge of honour. Her 'lunatic self-confidence' and single-minded focus on taking her pleasure made her narcissism fun and positive. When the SATC girls chatted about issues like anal sex etiquette and 'manscaping', the subtext of their discussions was frequently power. Despite being 'older', Kim Cattrall's Samantha lived by the motto that age is truly just a number . . . especially if you snagged it from some young hot stud.

Josephine Baker

Josephine Baker

Dancers express themselves with their bodies, which makes it only natural that they tend to gravitate toward fashions and lingerie that highlight their shape. Rare video footage of the legendary Josephine Baker's famous banana dance, taken in 1926 at the Folies-Bergère music hall in Paris, shows her performing as the 'savage' Fatou, dressed only in a heavily embellished bra, an impressive pile of shiny necklaces and a tutu made from palm fronds (which she typically alternated with a skirt of satin-covered bananas).

About that famous banana skirt

According to Josephine Baker's biographer, Jean-Claude, one of her adopted sons, his mother's famous costume was thought to have been designed by a certain Monsieur Christian, a companion of fashion designer Paul Poiret. A version of the costume most recently reappeared on singer Beyoncé at Fashion Rocks 2006 when she paid tribute to Josephine Baker by performing in a sparkly bra and banana skirt.

Clambering impishly down a giant felled tree and emerging from behind a tall tangle of upturned roots in the midst of a jungle scene, Fatou plops herself grandly centre stage in the splits. Preening in the direction of a jodhpur-clad white hunter who is reclining at the tree's base, she proceeds to undulate provocatively – and cheekily – in his direction, and then shimmies in a complete circle. Following a few bars of the Charleston, she finishes with a perky toss upward of her rump in his general direction.

A 'sinuous idol that enslaves and incites mankind', was how dance critic André Levinson described the experience of watching La Baker perform her famous dance. '[Hi]ps pressed together, one foot crossing the other, sticking out the behind and shaking your hands about', was how Ms Baker herself advised performing the Charleston. 'For too long people have hidden their behinds: they exist, I see no reason to be ashamed of them'. Of course, she also helped smash racial boundaries and stereotypes, and in the skimpiest of fruit ensembles.

Liza Minelli in *Cabaret*

'What good is sitting alone in your room? Come hear the music play. Life is a Cabaret, old chum. Come to the Cabaret.' Hearing these words automatically brings to mind Liza Minelli as Sally Bowles saucily

Achtung, fräulein!

'I got very inspired by Berlin. The whole 1920s thing, the Berlin Cabaret thing, the whole nightlife of Berlin in the '20s … And suddenly the word Fräulein came to mind. I thought it's such a great title, because it's all about women and celebrating them'.

Photographer Ellen Von Unwerth on her fashion and fetish photobook, *Fräulein* (Taschen, 2002)

straddling a chair in a bowler hat, black romper, and garters with stockings while performing at the seedy Kit Kat Klub in 1930s Berlin. Set during the decaying decadence of the end of the Weimar Republic, *Cabaret* was sort of an anti-musical, designed to make you feel distinctly uneasy and not-good. In this way, it was completely unlike Fosse's other lingerie-fest, Chicago, which was set during the violently glamorous Prohibition-era and involved prodigious amounts of scandal, social commentary and, of course, Cabaret-style undies.

The iconic Cabaret lingerie look is still influential today, especially in high-end lingerie brands such as La Perla (which has a Cabaret line) and in modern burlesque shows.

Punk rock

Punk performers have always enjoyed the racy side of life, and in their bid to challenge all forms of 'authority', many have titillated and often ended up nearly nude on-stage. And what better way to be undressed while dressed than in sexy underwear?

The outrageous punk singer Wendy O. Williams of the Plasmatics emerged from New York's 1970s punk scene, all smouldering looks, anger and of course, skimpy lingerie. Highlights of her career included an obscenity charge in Cleveland when Williams simulated sex on stage while wearing only shaving cream.

Lingerie inspired by the punk scene

Debbie Harry

Debbie Harry

Blonde punk goddess Debbie Harry was often compared to Marilyn Monroe, but with an anarchistic streak. 'It was a man's world – the good ol' boys chugging their guitars', she once told an interviewer. 'So we were really counterculture. And urban.' And barely dressed. Lingerie fits in with the punk aesthetic and assault on authority by helping the wearer reappropriate power. Showing skin on stage is a way of controlling the audience; female performers that are nude or scantily clad create a magnetism that draws the audience in and controls their energy and attention.

Lady Gaga in one of her many infamous, and often controversial costumes

Lady Gaga

The undisputed queen of lingerie-as-performance-art is currently Lady Gaga; in her live performances, public appearances and videos, she uses to lingerie to titillate and control her audience. Almost as interesting as her disdain of pants is her choice in collaborators, especially Jonas Åkerlund, who is somewhat infamous for his overt love of satanic imagery in the videos he directs. While his personal aesthetic may be controversial, he has also proved adept at balancing the image of a lingerie-clad Gaga as both erotic object and cold manipulator of the viewer in the tradition of male artists as diverse as Botticelli, Titian, Ingres, Courbet, Richard Avedon, and Helmut Newton

Examining the fame monster

Lady Gaga has based much of her image and career on her obsession with the nature of fame, but she also questions its addictive nature and heavy price-tag. At the 2010 MTV Video Music Awards, she performed Paparazzi, concluding the song by hanging from the ceiling and spinning, with blood covering her virginal-white lingerie.

'Celebrity life and media culture are probably the most overbearing pop-cultural conditions that we as young people have to deal with, because it forces us to judge ourselves', she has explained. 'I guess what I am trying to do is take the monster and turn the monster into a fairy tale.'

Gaga girdle gossip

After Lady Gaga performed in a skin-tight flesh-hued body suit, rumors flew: was it the same Kymaro Body Shaper 'as seen on TV' and late-night infomercials? Sadly for budget-strapped Gaga wannabes, no. However, for $39.99, it's still an extremely affordable way to get the look for more dash than cash.

Burlesque

As women have become more independent and economically powerful, they've begun to embrace their feminine side in some interesting ways. Unlike old-school feminists, post-modern 'powerful women' are simply exploring and expressing different facets of their personality. However, the degree to which our culture has become over-sexualised has reignited a desire to put some of the mystery back into sex.

Clad in lingerie and layers from demure to that worthy of a Vegas showgirl, adorned with miles of sparkles, feathers, and props, burlesque stars like Immodesty Blaize, Dita Von Teese, and Dirty Martini flaunt it with style to themed routines that are in equal part sexy, sassy, and humorous.

Playing at glamour

The word 'burlesque' is thought to possibly derive from the Italian for joke. It was popularised in Geoffrey Chaucer's *The Canterbury Tales* and has always enjoyed a humorous, often raunchy edge. Although associated these days with stripping – particularly in American burlesque – today's

Nice merkin!

'At home tonight making new Swarovski crystal pasties and a merkin, listening to The Presets. Crystal merkins are my new thing' wrote Dita Von Teese in one of her Twitter posts. An important item in any self-respecting burlesque star's lingerie lineup is her merkin, a cover for her pubic areas. Used as far back as the 17th century by prostitutes who were attempting to hide telltale syphilis lesions, its etymology is somewhat surprising. The name Mary as in Mary Magdalen, may indicate a possible prostitute; from Mary comes various words for slatternly women and sluts: moll, as in gun moll and Moll Flanders, which eventually became malkin, the probable origin of merkin.

Burlesque or just xxx

When does burlesque become
so sexy, that it crosses the
line into being stripping with
props? 'The current strip clubs
are a lot closer to the original
environment and performance
intention of the "original"
burlesque than the neo-
burlesque shows of today',
explains Bombshell Betty.
'Women and men get dressed
up in extremely extravagant
costumes to perform for mixed
audiences in shows at an
assortment of venues – from
dive bars to large theatres.
Most of the performers do
this as a moderately expensive
hobby, for the love of it and
few performers actually make
a living at it. Many acts are
as much performance art as
striptease, and the focus is
much more on theatricality
and personality than it is
on body parts. While most
burlesque acts involve some
stripping, not all of them do,
and different performers who
do strip only take off as much
or as little as they want to. The
feeling at these shows is usually
boisterous and celebratory.'

popular burlesque tends to be a lighthearted celebration of sexiness rather than seediness. While camp, there is usually a satirical edge, a touch of irony and a good deal of raw talent and woman-friendliness. 'They are attracted by the message I bring', Dita Von Teese has pointed out. 'You can play dressing up with elegance or make a striptease for your significant other. The essence of burlesque is about dressing up properly, enjoying glamour, and taking more time for yourself'.

Few items of clothing can make a woman feel sexier than really hot lingerie, which is at the heart of the most successful burlesque routines. According to Immodesty Blaize: 'I actually think the genre of burlesque appeals to women as much, if not more, than men. I think the glamour really appeals and also the show is done in such a theatrical way, and it's such a huge spectacle, this fantasy unfolding before your eyes, with those elements and those really erotic undertones, it definitely means that the performers are very much glorified as women, rather than objectified'.

Lingerie in the graphic arts and pop culture

Close-fitting and close to the body, lingerie lends itself to fantasy interpretations better than any other garment. Superheroes such as Wonder Woman have worn outfits that were no more than exotic underwear with pride as have sci-fi heroines and most recently those inhabitants of a virtual world, avatars. Models in lingerie have been an inspiration for photographers such as Helmut Newton and Guy Bourdin, whose imagery often tipped over into voyeurism. In popular culture, a fascination with lingerie's ability to transform the body has led to a recent resurgence of interest in corsetry and the practice of tight-lacing.

Milla Jovovich in a
costume designed by
Jean Paul Gaultier

Wonder Woman

Spreading the doctrine of peace, love, and equality, Wonder Woman was conceived as a role model for girls. She was inspired by a psychologist and early feminist, Dr William Marston, who was worried that in a culture pervaded by violent and misogynistic superheroes, young girls lacked women whom they could emulate. DC Comics hired Marston in 1941 to help create the first female superhero, an Amazonian princess sent by the goddess Aphrodite to spread the word of peace, love and sexual equality, not by brute force but by reason and reform. Her towering build and flawless physique were showcased by her bustier bodysuit, perfect for apprehending villains with sexy panache, but with no trailing capes or skirts to get in the way when engaging in hand-to-hand combat.

Cyberpunk, anime and 1970s Japanese cinema

The creative influence of Japanese manga and anime has long been a fertile source of lingerie imagery, including Luc Besson's 1997 *The Fifth Element* starring Milla Jovovich in costumes by Jean Paul Gaultier, and *Ghost in the Shell* (1995) chronicling the activities of a counter-terrorist outfit in futuristic Japan, both of which feature heroines in bondage-style lingerie. Clearly, performing full-on kung fu and hand-to-hand combat would be difficult in a bustier and thigh-high boots, but it's meant to be fantasy. Many women feel their most sexy – and, therefore, powerful – in great lingerie, so by referencing the source of their feminine power, it makes the heroines' crimefighting lingerie ensembles make sense on a certain level.

Referencing the kimono

An earlier cinematic influence from Japan also provides an interesting twist on lingerie: the elegantly sexy kimono robe worn by the heroines of blood-drenched action movies which provide a visually arresting juxtaposition of the serene robe against the violence of the wearer. Starting in the 1970s, Japan's Pinky Violence genre – which includes classics like *Zero Woman: Red Handcuffs*, *The Most Dangerous Game*, *Lady Snowblood: Love Song of Vengeance*, and *The Razor: Sword of Justice* – unleashed a memorable torrent of arthouse imagery, grindhouse violence, and strong female characters who made the glamorous kimonos they fought in seem simultaneously erotic and exotic, and, possibly, a little dangerous. They are perfect for the femme fatale lead in a Quentin Tarantino flick (like the über-glamorous Lucy Liu as the gorgeous but murderous, samurai sword-wielding crime boss O-Ren Ishii in 2003's *Kill Bill*) or just a ordinary girl looking to create an air of mystery with her lingerie, with just a peek of skin here or a seductive flash of thigh there.

Date my sexy avatar

you wanna date my avatar?' sings the cute gamer girl in exy, avatar-fabulous gear. 'She's a star, and she's hotter reality by far / You'll never see my actual face. Our love, ove with be in a virtual space / Be anything you want o be. And if you think I'm not the one, log off, log off d we'll be done'. Do You Wanna Date My Avatar is an e video created by and starring the same female role-ng gamer who created *The Guild* (WatchTheGuild.com), ward-winning online sitcom comprised of 3-8 minute sodes about a community of avid online role-playing rs. The video stars the cast members, each dressed as avatar; the series is so popular, the day of its general se on iTunes, it reached number one, and within two was viewed on YouTube more than 1 million times.

Lingerie in advertising

Andy Warhol believed that advertising was an art form: 'When you think about it, department stores are kind of like museums', he once noted. Semi-naked women in their undies could easily be compared to the glamorous women depicted by Botticelli and Delacroix. The reason that sexy women are used to sell products is that everyone loves looking at them. Rather than a symbol of the woman's commodification, it is actually a sign of the power of the female form and its ability to sell whatever product is associated with it.

Ad campaign by Berlei

In love with life...
in love with Berlei Sarong-Plus

The girdles that go with a wonderful life — Sarong-Plus! Because they let you move in the nicest way. Cool Lycra has gentle, summer-weight control that keeps every curve in place, while you delight in the freedom of Sarong's criss-cross front. There's a Sarong-Plus design for every figure—light-weight Junior, 2" waist-accent Sarong, the smooth hi-waister, and the sleek corselet. 1" waist Sarong-Plus Junior, from 69/6; 2" waist-control Sarong-Plus, from 79/6; Hi-waisted pull-on, from 99/6; Sleek corselet, contoured cups, 159/6; Criss-cross bras in heavenly lace, 42/6.

 LOOK FOR THE GIRL WITH THE BERLEI BADGE

WOMAN'S DAY with WOMAN, November 29

Advertising itself has become a commodity to be consumed and like any commodity being sold, a hefty dose of sex appeal makes the message come across much more easily. When polled about special issues of fashion magazines like the September issue, a study found that almost 1 in 4 of the readers ignored the editorial content to focus solely on the fashion advertisements, while 82 per cent recalled ad spreads of up to six pages.

Great ad campaigns

A particularly memorable lingerie-in-advertising moment was *White Wedding*, a six-part webisode series in spring 2008 for Agent Provocateur Bridal, shot by Nick Knight and starring Kate Moss. Moss was first depicted as virginal and soft in a sweet white bustier and stockings, but as each succeeding episode delves into the fallacies and hypocrisies of weddings today and unravels the 'religious organisation behind it', she begins her descent: first into despair, then as a knife-wielding Bridezilla intent on revenge and finally, in a red bra and panties as a kind of dangerous pagan goddess presiding over a pit of fire with a jarring Jimi Hendrix-like guitar accompaniment.

Another great ad by Agent Provocateur

The suggestive power of lingerie

Lingerie in art, photography and pulp fiction

Lingerie has long been a staple of porn, striptease and soft-core, probably ever since belly dancers started shimmying suggestively in an attempt to tempt an over-stimulated sultan in their bejewelled bras and semi-transparent harem skirts. Keeping at least part of the body hidden adds to the lure of the chase, the pursuit, while suggestively removing it is the essence of seduction; together, they create that sexy sizzle. 'I love all the old pictures – of spanking and Bettie Page and corsets', photographer Ellen Von Unwerth once remarked in an interview about her work. 'The mystery in my pictures differentiates them from porn.'

Helmut Newton

In a typical Helmut Newton photograph, the men are usually dressed, often in a suit, while the women are seminude, clad in sexy-stern lingerie and mistresswear. However, the men, with their naked desire, look oddly vulnerable and the women firmly in control. 'First of all, why would I spend my life with women, whether they are dressed or undressed, if I didn't like women?' Newton once pointed out. 'Another thing is that in all the photographs, the women are triumphant and the men are just toys. They are just accessories and always servile to the women.'

Sexploitation in poster art

Sexploitation

From a cultural perspective, sexploitation and soft-core films are more than just an excuse for sexy babes to strut around in, and then strip off skimpy lingerie; they also address how we define beauty and help shape desire. They are simultaneously an avenue of discourse on sex and a 'fantasy machine'. Painter John Currin's scantily clad women are often inspired both by the girlie, lingerie-clad pages of *Playboy* and sexploitation flicks from the 1950s and 1960s, which typically featured sexy violence and lingerie clad robo-babes, especially the women-in-prison genre.

Pulp fiction

A longtime source of titillating lingerie imagery was on the covers of inexpensive novels that were commonly sold during the first half of the 20th century on newspaper stands and at corner stores. The covers of these potboilers reflected their content: lurid, seedy, exploitive and often devoted to dames in distress, in compromising positions, in revealing lingerie and whenever possible, in all three. Much like the covers of today's porn DVDs, the book's artwork teased people into buying them. Pulp tales with themes such as forbidden love, especially pre-martial sex and lesbian erotica – were usually penned by straight men using female

A scantily clad damsel in distress

pseudonyms and writing for a male audience and they often included numerous scenes of gratuitous graphic sex.

Inspiration for high art

Cheap and trashy as it was, pulp was popular, reflecting what people wanted – which is why it later inspired Richard Prince's *Nurse* series of images in 2006. Prince scanned various pulp covers, printed them out onto canvases, and further altered them with acrylic paint. Runaway Nurse, in particular, looks fabulous in her naughty lingerie as she poses at the end of a bed against a brass bed frame, her hair coiffed in 1940s sausage roll curls, nurse's hat and surgical mask still on and top unbuttoned to reveal a strapless black bra.

Jeff Koons' *Made in Heaven*

Pop artist Jeff Koons similarly used a pulp art approach to maximum effect in *Made in Heaven*, a series he presented at the 1990 Venice Biennale. The paintings depicted the artist himself nude and having sex with his then wife, Italian porn star (and one-time member of parliament) Cicciolina, who was clad in a pretty white bustier and stockings. Koons explained

Naughty nurses on the runway

For his Louis Vuitton Spring 2008 collection, designer Marc
Jacobs sent models Stephanie Seymour, Eva Herzigova,
Nadja Auermann, and Naomi Campbell down the runway
dressed as sexy but kinky nurses in see-through plastic coats,
their underwear clearly visible beneath. Inspired by Richard
Prince's *Nurse* paintings, Jacobs consciously appropriated
Prince's appropriation, adding that it is 'fine, so long as there
are three differences in everything!'

Heaven as a representation of a modern Adam and Even, noting: 'I had to go to the depths of my own sexuality, my own morality, to be able to remove fear, guilt and shame from myself. All of this has been removed from the viewer.'

Like pulp, Heaven directly bypasses the polite part of the brain, and in combination with our newest social obsession, fame, plays on people's voyeuristic impulse to see the famous in flagrante. This is especially true if the subjects of the paintings are taken into consideration: while Cicciolina is unquestionably pretty, Koons is obviously more eye-of-the-beholder attractive.

Ex-porn star, Cicciolina

The transformative power of lingerie
Mr Pearl, corsetier extraordinaire

While men have corseted at various times throughout history for 'medicinal' purposes (back support) and for vanity (shapewear), more recently, a subset has been tightlacing for erotic stimulation. Renowned corsetier to couturiers including Jean Paul Gaultier, Christian Lacroix, Thierry Mugler, and John Galliano, South African-born Mr Pearl has himself worn a corset for years. He reflects, 'To wear the corset all the time, the way I do, is my true discipline. To be tied all the time – as I am – one is best when left tied. Except when you bathe of course. I am always tied. It is very odd now to be loose – to be loose, to leave the laces even slightly untied is wrong – one feels unnatural, incomplete. It is essential to always wear the corset very tight and well-tied. We understand the tying of the bow denotes possession. The gentleman who has the pleasure of tying the final bow owns you.'

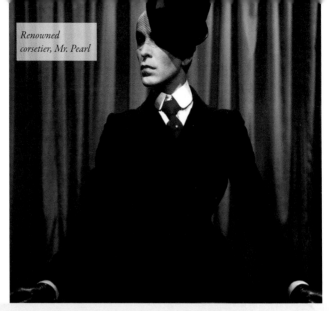

Renowned corsetier, Mr. Pearl

The exquisite joys of tightlacing

'In the beginning of my discipline I experienced it as a euphoria and more often than I do now. Now I am only comfortable, and I am uncomfortable without the corset. I see this trance-state in others now; in the beginning, a kind of claustrophobia overtakes them, that in extreme situations leads to a faint. It depends on their level. We seek a kind of sustained euphoria that may take you by surprise – we call it the Corset Moment. You cannot take anymore – cannot go forward – but neither can you withdraw. Now that you have started, you must and you will go on. This sensation I might liken to a roller coaster – fear, even terror, then exhilaration. The corset has taken you over, you cannot think of anything else. It takes over your mind. Your whole being is now subject to its embrace …To have smelling-salts on hand is a good idea. But I must say to loosen the corset at that Moment is a bad idea. One must pass through it, emerge through discipline.'

Corsetier Mr Pearl on the 'ecstatic' trance that occurs when corseting for extended periods.

Post-surgery lingerie

Enough women are similarly self-altering that the lingerie firm, Le Mystère introduced No. 9, a collection of bras designed specifically for breasts that had been augmented through surgery. Teaming up with a certified plastic surgeon, the firm's designers compiled years of clinical observation, measurements and complaints from women unable to find attractive bras that fit their new contours (and style sensibilities) and combined them into a flattering, fashionable post-surgery product.

At the other end of the surgery spectrum, mastectomy patients have traditionally used prosthetics to create the illusion of breast symmetry. Product designer Mary Huibregtse re-thought the mastectomy bra for her graduation project in 2004 at the Design Academy Eindhoven with her '½ Bras' that are sleek and modern, and celebrate the wearer's post-surgical asymmetry.

Plus-size lingerie

Ancient Egyptian art depicts a nation of slender and stylish folk when, in fact, a significant portion of their society didn't conform to that

When DDD still isn't busty enough

American tabloid-fixture Heidi Montag extended her 15 minutes of fame by going under the knife in a surgical marathon that included 10 procedures including liposuction on her legs and back, a brow lift, botox in her forehead, a nose job touchup, chin reduction, neck liposuction, having her ears pinned back, fat injection in her cheeks, and of course, enormous breast implants. 'Triple D isn't big enough', she has been quoted as saying about her new measurements which are becoming similar to Barbie's proportions, were she human (5'9' and 36-18-33).

ideal at all. Looking at today's similarly deceptive fashion magazines, populated as they are by tall, willowy, ultra-slender mannequins, will anthropologists in the distant future make the same assumptions about us? The fact is that many real women today are shorter, curvier and more similar in body-type to celebrities including the singer Adele, plus-size model Crystal Renn, and in many cases, Beth Ditto. And the market for lingerie is finally starting to cater to voluptuous women.

Plus-size glamour

Non stick-figured celebrities have helped promote the acceptance of plus-size sexiness. Queen Latifah launched her Curvation line of fashion and

Plus-size lingerie can
be just as sexy

lingerie when she couldn't find intimate apparel that was both plus-size and pretty, while voluptuous diva Jill Scott found herself so annoyed with the abysmal state of bras for bigger girls, that she approached plus-size fashion emporium Ashley Stewart to devise a solution.

'Enough is enough, so we created the Butterfly Bra', she explains about the novel design which eliminates shoulder-grooving, unsightly bulges, back fat and 'all that foolishness we've been putting up with since our mothers' mothers' mothers had a bra ... I know that when I'm wearing the Butterfly bra, I feel taller. I feel freer. I feel happier. I don't have to deal with all of that internal drama. I spend more time out, I have more fun. I dance more often, because I don't feel the weight and the pressure of my beautiful breasts. I love them, I don't want to have surgery ... No more harnesses! No more grandma bras! Something that makes you feel sexy, lovely, and supported, and comfortable.'

Fashionable curves

Even high-end fashion magazines like *Vogue Italia* and *Elle* are starting to recognise that beauty comes in all shapes. 'Between the recent launch of the Vogue Curvy site and now French *Elle*'s first plus-size issue, it gives more validation that plus-size is making its way into the high-fashion world', confirms Nancy LeWinter, the editorial director of

OneStopPlus.com, one of the largest online sources of lingerie for plus-sized women who want fashionable undies. 'These significant steps show the acceptance and praise of plus-size women, and is yet another example of the ways in which plus size women are being empowered and respected as trendsetters in the industry, as much as their size 0 counterparts.'

Plus-size corset from 'hips and curves'

The 'Red Hot Fantasy' bra,
by Victoria's Secret

Angels in lingerie

'What used to be part of a woman's trousseau has come out of the hope chest', points out pop culture critic Robert Thompson. 'Now, underwear is designed to be seen and worn on the outside'. It is the featured attraction at the most watched 'fashion' show in the world as the Victoria's Secret 'Angels' parade down the runway in sexy undies. This lavish event usually features one Angel in a bejeweled bra-and-panty set; the $15 million price tag on the bra worn by Gisèle Bündchen in 2000 found it a place in the *Guinness Book of World Records* as the most expensive lingerie ever.

Football in underwear

Such is the enthusiasm for hot chicks in lingerie, that in 2004, the 'Lingerie Bowl' premiered during the American Super Bowl halftime entertainment: two seven-woman teams playing American football clad only in protective padding and lingerie. It proved so popular, it grew into an actual league, with camp names like Philadelphia Passion, Miami Caliente, Dallas Desire, LA Temptation and San Diego Seduction. No doubt the requirement that Lingerie Football League players not wear anything additional under their official uniform (or face a $500 fine for doing so) helps, as the players are required to sign a contract that they 'knowingly and voluntarily' agree to the accidental nudity that occurs when their uniforms are ripped off or pulled down during play.

Lingerie Football League

Accidental exposure?

The trend toward accidental-on-purpose nudity most recently gained momentum during the 2004 American Super Bowl halftime show. As part of a song-medley with Janet Jackson, Justin Timberlake promised to have 'you naked by the end of this song' during *Rock Your Body*; standing behind Jackson, he reached around and dramatically pulled off the part of her costume covering her right breast. Despite the fact she was wearing a nipple cover, the so-called 'wardrobe malfunction' provoked weird amounts of public outrage and landed the network airing the game with a $550,000 fine.

It also kicked off a brave new mini-era in underwear-optional moments. From Britney Spears to Paris Hilton, Amy Winehouse, Lindsay Lohan, Rihanna, Lily Allen, Nadine Coyle of Girls Aloud, Helena Bonham Carter, all women long in the glare of the fame spotlight (and who probably should have known better), all have been photographed upskirt and sans panties, with side boob, nip slips and tops that end up completely see-through under the glare of camera flashes.

Janet Jackson and Justin Timberlake performing at the 2004 American Super Bowl

Syria's extraordinary lingerie culture

The opposite of the public exposure of underwear or more is without doubt the burqa, and yet, in Syria, a peek underneath this all-encompassing

Syria's secret passion

garment reveals a world of lingerie at its most eye-popping. From 'curtain bras' that draw open at the touch of a remote, to angel outfits with wings, to G-strings with attached toy mobile phones, lingerie in Syria is notorious throughout the Middle East.

Embellished with everything from faux fur to fake flowers to feathered birds, lights, fake scorpions and even music-emitting, it is displayed openly in the souks and also includes edible underwear in fruit flavours and S&M inflected concoctions. It reflects partly folk tradition (lingerie is an important component of the trousseau) and partly the focus on the family – because a good sex life is, well, good for everyone.

Mistress of men

Syria's notorious lingerie has sparked more than a few debates about whether it turns women into human sex toys or is simply an effective way to keep marriages exciting and intact. 'They're not supposed to be sexually stimulating to other people, but at home, to the husband, they're supposed to provoke his sexuality and dress in the manner that will attract him and do whatever he says', says Ammar Abdulhamid, a Syrian writer and dissident based in the US. At the same time, though, 'it gives women a lot of control. Women can use sexuality to manipulate men.'

Aubade's Japanese
themed collection

Japanese naughtiness

Even more at peace with their love of everything naughty are the Japanese. While teaching English near Tokyo, photographer Joan Sinclair heard about private Japanese men's clubs with mirrored floors and fantasy décor, and one day, a friend finally took her on a tour of Kabukicho, the country's biggest red-light district. 'I was blown away', she recalled. 'There were train clubs with all-you-can-grope commuting women. And fake hospitals, where the customer can lie in bed and get 'treated' by a pantiless nurse'.

She documented the scene in *Pink Box: Inside Japan's Sex Clubs*, a photobook of 155 full-colour photos of the anything-goes Japanese sex and kink industry. The title was inspired by the fact that pink is the Japanese euphemism for the commercial sex trade, and the 'Pink Box' is a private dancer's room in the back of a well-known Osaka club. A combination of charm and persistence finally gained Sinclair entry to shoot in 90 different clubs – a tiny fraction in the country's second largest industry after automobiles.

Not really underground

Interestingly, the industry only seems underground to foreigners because they are typically denied access, apparently for five main reasons: '1.

Foreigners don't understand the rules – of which there are admittedly many. 2. They scare the Japanese customers. 3. They complain too much. 4. They can't communicate well with the women if the women get uncomfortable. 5. They may have AIDS'.

An extremely popular service is the 'Sexual Harassment Office' where the customer can select the style of tights that he wants the woman to wear; choices include beige, black or sparkly, or, alternatively, fishnet tights and panties. He then gets to rip it off the 'secretary' and for an extra $20, he can keep them. 'The schoolgirl, the commuting secretary – the women you see every day – are forbidden fruit … These clubs allow people to break the social rules, using everyday archetypes', says Sinclair. As one of the men she interviewed admitted: 'I think all men are universally perverted; it's just that in Japan we do something about it'.

Fetish-style bra straps

Sheer bra

Innerwear anytime: lingerie in the 21st century

It seemed at one time that properly glamorous underwear was reserved only for special occasions and the boudoir. But over the past 15 years or so there has been an explosion in the availability of gorgeous lingerie at every price point. In department stores, chain stores and even at the super-budget end of the market, women can buy appealing underwear that fits and supports better than ever. There's no excuse for a grey bra and saggy knickers when you can wear something pretty and matching for less than £10. And as women's bust sizes have increased, manufacturers have kept up with them, producing bras to fit almost everyone.

Satin bra, sheer trim

Cute lingerie gets affordable

While advances in fabric technology have continued to make modern lingerie more comfortable, better fitting and ever more high-performance, the selection of sexy undies available at every price point has never been as plentiful. This is partly thanks to mass-market retailers who have made it possible for even women on the tightest of budgets to indulge in a little lingerie luxury. In the U.K., Marks & Spencer's 'Worn to be Seen' range of slinky slips and lace-panelled bodies makes it easy to imbue any outfit in your wardrobe with a lingerie feel for around £35, or, perhaps, to splurge on something delectable by *Collette by Collette Dinnigan* for less than the price of dinner for two in London or New York. At John Lewis, women can indulge in retro lingerie glam at retro prices, in particular, the pointy 1950s-inspired Fantasie Belle bras. A spokesman for the store remarked, 'Throughout the last century the trend for feminine pointy shaped bras experienced a renaissance following times of a toughened economy, marking a return of unabashed femininity as women seek to have more fun with fashion as a form of escapism.'

Changing shapes

These days, an increasing number of us work out regularly and few things show off gym-toned abs and diet-disciplined derrières to greater effect than a sheer bra and panty set. For those of us who have continued to increase in size, either through over-indulgence or plastic surgery, underwear has thankfully followed suit. The leading department store, Selfridges, has observed that since 2005, bras with cup sizes in the D to G range have been selling at 50 per cent more each year. They recently introduced Fantasie's K-cup size (and if you were wondering, the circumference of

Andres Sardá bikini

the band is over four feet [122 cm], with each cup measuring 18 inches [46 cm] at its widest).

Innerwear on the outside

Innerwear-as-outerwear has also been a strong – and ongoing – trend and racy lingerie is no longer exclusively for the boudoir. Wearing a glamorous corset with a pair of jeans – or, as shown by Bottega Veneta in Spring 2010 with city shorts and a blazer – is a chic way to add some spice to an otherwise ordinary day look.

Some pieces are just too fabulous to keep under wraps. From sassy colours and prints, to oversize saucy satin bows or floral rosettes at the back, and puffy layers of fluffy tulle and lace, a new generation of designers

Strumpet and Pink - crochet panties

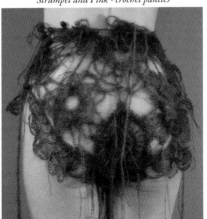

*Cut-out panties by
Mint Siren*

are applying their skills specifically to lingerie, rather than considering it as an afterthought. Designers such as Chantal Thomass, Carine Gilson, Damaris, and Strumpet and Pink have brought a handcrafted, almost artisanal feel to the field. In some cases, it is as if grandma had been inspired by punk rock and cobbled together a tatted, knitted deconstruction chic version of her beloved granny panty – in a fierce lipstick red.

And besides, when you've splurged on a £3,000 confection by Damaris, why would you want to keep it hidden? Certainly not if it's the rock star-worthy $1500 feathered girdle from Bordelle or more 'modestly' priced £365 'Angela Cage' bandage creation (also by Bordelle) that sold out at Selfridges within 24 hours after singer Rihanna had performed in something similar at the 2009 American Music Awards.

Lingerie on the catwalk

A number of highly influential designers have continued to slip dresses, lacy overlays and sheers down the runway for several seasons now. They are increasingly inventive about taking super-sexy lingerie and making it work in an everyday chic kind of way, whether layered over tees, sweaters, button down shirts, or tucked cheekily under a menswear-style blazer.

Marc Jacobs Spring/ Summer 2010

In the Spring 2010 collections, all-out boudoir chic was a catwalk mainstay, from earthy black bustier and matching lace skirted señoritas at Dolce & Gabbana, to a coquettish bride wearing a white bra and panties – and not much else – at Vivienne Westwood, VPL's Parisienne sophisticate in low-slung black harem pants and a black sports bra/cropped bustier under her boyish blazer and of course Jean Paul Gaultier revisiting (again!) his signature rocket-cone bra in a grandma-approved satiny peach hue, paired with black sheer stockings and garters peeking out from slouchy tap pants cum city shorts.

One of the most interesting intersections of innerwear, outerwear and innerwear-as-outerwear was undoubtedly at Marc Jacobs. From loose harem-style pants and flat Arabian Nights slippers, to a chocolate brown 1970s sweater, modern hipster-dude scarf, hippie fringe bag, and cartoony pair of space-age topknots sprouting from the model's head – the ensemble was a platter of sartorial appropriation from other eras, cultures and mediums.

But what really got fashion tongues wagging was the lingerie. Rather than peeking out demurely, it was the full-on focal point of the ensemble: a high-waisted nylon granny panty pulled right over the sweater and all the way up to the natural waist, a mere few inches below the shiny satin bullet bra worn on the outside of the sweater. Odd, yes, but infinitely intriguing. The effect? A chic postmodern, time-travelling magpie – with really eclectic taste in undies.

Pearl thong by Bracli

Choosing, buying and caring for your lingerie

It really is true that well-fitting lingerie can make or break an outfit – and these days can literally transform a woman's figure, and greatly increase the kinds of clothes she can wear. A wide range of sizes (bras can now be found in cup sizes that range from AAA to KK) means that almost everyone should be able to find a bra that fits and flatters. Beautiful lingerie has become mainstream, and even budget stores now carry appealing matching sets. At the luxury end of the market there is a huge choice of exquisitely crafted lingerie that blends the latest designs with the finest fabrics.

Tips from the top

To get the correct fit and care for your lingerie properly, try some of these tips from stylist Tina Gill.

1 Have a professional bra fitting The reason that so many women wear the wrong size bra is that they are wearing a cup size that is too small with a band that is too loose. If you raise your arms above your head and find your bra is sliding up, the band is too big to provide any support. A bra fitting with a profession fitter once a year will ensure you continue to wear the correct size. Remember that great-fitting clothes start with perfectly fitting undergarments.

2 Build a lingerie wardrobe Choose a colour theme such as black or brown and start with a few separates that can be mixed and matched in a variety of ways; some coordinating pyjama pants and robe will help create a 'working lingerie wardrobe'. Then add in some tops in a variety of fun colours such as turquoise or hot pink for variety.

3 The essentials A sexy camisole, slip or nightie that's cut on the bias in a satiny fabric hides lumps and bumps and flows flatteringly over and away from the body. A cotton nightie with sexy touches like a plunging neckline or peekaboo cutouts provides a good balance of bombshell and comfort.

4 The 'life is short' piece A corset! It flatters every body type, keeps your tummy tucked in, gives the breasts a lift and the lacing makes it easy to fake an hourglass figure. It also creates a longer, leaner torso in order to make you appear even thinner. Rock this versatile piece in the bedroom with panties and stockings, or out on the town with a pair of dark denim jeans and a boyfriend blazer.

5 Have fun Keep trying on lingerie until you find pieces that make you feel like a million dollars and then buy them! You're guaranteed to feel sexy and confident as you heat things up in the boudoir.

Lingerie set by Etam

Choosing the correct size

Eight out of every 10 women are wearing the wrong sized bra. If the straps slide off your shoulders or the band creeps up in the back between your shoulder blades, your bra band size is too large according to Rachel LeRoy of the lingerie blog Intimate Guide: What to Wear Under There (IntimateGuide.com). Remember the days when pesky boys would 'snap' your bra in school? If your bra band pulls out more than two inches, it's either too big or fastened too loosely. 'Because the band supports the breasts and breast tissue will stretch out over time, causing the dreaded droop,' warns LeRoy. The tightness of your bra band is directly related to how perky breasts will appear.

EVER REGRET A NIGHT OUT
...UNPREPARED?

Lingerie solutions to modern problems

Problem: An impromptu hook-up materialises.
Solution: Always keep a purse-sized overnight kit tucked in your handbag! It should contain a condom, travel toothbrush and mini-toothpaste, towelette and best of all, a cute pair of clean undies. And be sure to never leave home without at least one package of Flingwear on your person; each teeny three-inch water-resistant package contains a pair of non-creep, non-show cotton panties. (Flingwear.com)

Problem: You love your shapewear, but you have a hot date.
Solution: The Yummie Tummie Teddie. Sexy lace disguises the fact this bodysuit is actually slimming and shaping on the sly, so it's not embarrassing to be seen in. (YummieTummie.com)

Problem: Your man has love handles.
Solution: Man Spanx! A cotton compression undershirt that firms, flattens and says 'game on!' (Spanx.com)

Problem: Your cups runneth over – whenever you do any kind of sport.
Solution: The as-seen-on-Oprah Enell Sports Bra. A super-snug, slightly complicated affair that hooks up the front and can take a while to put on, but once you do, you'll be hooked for good. (Enell.com)

Problem: In a world of let-it-all-hang-out, you're a pin-up girl at heart.
Solution: Although the idea of vintage lingerie is lovely, however, it's probably best when it comes to undies to buy new. PinUpGirlClothing.com sells vintage reproduction black bullet bras and girdles with garter hooks – and at relatively retro prices.

Lingerie names you should know

Lingerie should be as individual as you are. Here are some choice picks of lingerie we love, from both well known designers and a few who are a little off the beaten track.

Agent Provocateur An opulent range of inspired creations designed to intensify life's pleasures and unlock inner desires. Designed with both the boardroom and the boudoir in mind. (AgentProvocateur.com)

Atsuko Kudo Winner of the European Fetish Award's 2008/9 Best Fetish Design and designer of Beyoncé's curve-enhancing buttercup yellow dress in the Lady Gaga video for Telephone. Couture latex design and accessories for the bedroom, the club, the salon and beyond. (AtsukoKudo.com)

Aubade Specialists in the perfect boudoir accoutrements for the French art of loving: seduction, complicity and humour. (Aubade.com)

Britta Uschkamp Saucy lingerie with punk rockin' 'n' rolling sensibilities. (BrittaUschkamp.com)

Buttress & Snatch What today's pin-up wants to wear underneath it all. Handmade in London using silks, vintage trims and fun retro prints. (ButtressAndSnatch.co.uk)

Cadolle Corsetiere Herminie Cadolle helped free women from constrictive lingerie when she showed the bra she had invented at the 1889 Exposition in Paris. Today, a fifth generation family member, Poupie Cadolle, presides over the fancy French line of lingerie, bustiers and sexy shapewear. (Cadolle.com)

Great moments in modern lingerie

1901 Invention of the Gibson Girl S-bend corset

1908 The long line corset slims hips

1914 The bathing beauty makes her debut

1920 Flapper girls of the Jazz Age bind their breasts

1926 Garters hold up stockings (and keep the Prohibition era sexy)

1935 The modern ABCD bra sizing system is introduced

1940 Nylon stockings become available in the US

1946 Louis Reard scandalises Paris with the first bikini

1949 Military-inspired Bullet bras are the height of fashion

1956 Brigitte Bardot is pictured in a bikini

1957 Tights are invented

1963 Rudi Gernreich designs the Monokini

1976 Charlie's Angels make TV crime-fighting sexy (and jiggly)

1980 Brooke Shields lets nothing come between her and her Calvin Klein jeans

1982 Lingerie gets a fitness makeover thanks to the aerobics craze

1983 Flashdance and Fame introduce the legwarmer to everyone

1984 Madonna is pictured in a bustier

1989 Claudia Schiffer is photographed in a bustier for Guess

1990 Gaultier designs a cone bra for Madonna's Blonde Ambition tour

1992 Calvin Klein launches ad with Marky Mark and Kate Moss in undies

1992 Victoria's Secret is no longer a secret

1994 Courtney Love sings in her Kinderwhore baby doll nightie

1994 The Wonderbra goes global

1997 A&F Bruce Weber sell clothes with undies on

2000+ New millennium Lady Gaga takes over the world in fabulous lingerie

Erotic design by Maison Close

Carine Gilson Fine French silk and Chantilly lace confections made by hand in Belgium. Simply exquisite! (CarineGilson.com)

Chantal Thomass With her severe black Louise Brooks bob, crimson lips and all-black wardrobe, the lingerie designer is as recognisable as her glamorous lingerie creations which veil and reveal the body with lace and sensual transparent fabrics and frilly frippery. (ChantalThomass.fr)

Charnos A British brand that recently celebrated 50 years in the business. (Charnos.co.uk)

Claire Pettibone Where modern princesses and magnificent goddesses go to stock up on lacy slips and delicate underthings. (ClairePettibone.com)

Damaris When 25-year-old St Martin's graduate Damaris Evans first showed her signature bow knickers with 'cheeky' bottom cleavage to the lingerie buyers at Selfridges and Le Bonne Marche in Paris in 2001, they snapped up the new luxury line,

despite retail prices ranging from £125-£3,000. Known for its fine silks, satins, chiffons and even snakeskin adorned with gold lamé, pom-poms, feathers, Swarovski Crystals – and, for select private customers, real diamonds. Its younger, more wearable sister-line is Mimi Holliday. (Damaris.co.uk)

Elle McPherson Intimates The Australian supermodel invests her eponymous line of lingerie with fit, function and fashionable design. (ElleMacphersonIntimates.com)

Elise Anderegg Paris Stylish, seductive pieces for day or night, including delicate lace-trimmed camis, tap pants in rich hues and frilly, feminine touches. (EliseAnderegg.com)

Elise Aucouturier A former designer for Christian Dior, Marithé et François Girbaud and a number of Vanity Fair brands, Elise is known for her modern, elegant and undeniably French designs. (EliseAucouturier.com)

Hips and Curves

A guide to plus-size lingerie

There are more and more places for girls with curves to find sexy pieces that fit and flatter, including robes, nighties, babydolls, negligees, fishnets and garters, thigh-highs, glamorous corsets, camisoles and flirty ruffled boy-shorts. Here are some to try:

Ashley Stewart
AlwaysForMe.com
AboutCurves.com
Avenue.com
AmpleBosom.com
BiggerBras.com
BrasToGo.com.au
BigGalsLingerie.com
Curvation.com
HerRoom.com
HipsAndCurves.com
AlwaysForMe.com
LaneBryant.com
LingerieExotique.com
Torrid
Junonia.com
Figuresque.com
Kiyonna
Frederick's of Hollywood
OhSoCurvy.com
OneStopPlus.com
Sexy-Lingerie.co.uk
PlusSizePlum.com
Silhouettes.com

Eres Synonymous with jetsetting luxury lingerie and swimwear and renowned for flattering fit and innovative cuts. (EresParis.com)

Falke The last word in luxury hosiery and tights that sculpt, shape and last. (Falke.com)

Fifi Chachnil A girlie, glamorous blend of influences including music, romance, fashion and theater. (FifiChachnil.com)

Fleur of England Owner Fleur Turner uses fabrics and trims sourced from all over the world and crafts them in the UK and EU into her award-winning and stylish bras, panties and slips. (FleurOfEngland.com)

Frankly Darling A hip London brand featuring a froufrouteuse line of retro lingerie. (Petite-Coquette.co.uk)

Gatez-Moi Classically coquettish lingerie from Tokyo. (Gatez-Moi.com)

Gentry de Paris Cashmere knickers and luxurious chemises. (GentryDeParis.com)

Guia La Bruna An Italian designer with a French fille feel whose designs showed up in bed on Charlotte on Sex and the City. (GuiaLaB.com)

Jean Yu Futuristic yet retro lingerie that's perfect for cyberbabes. (AtelierJeanYu.com)

Jenna Leigh For the glamour girl who doesn't want to keep her undies under wraps. (JennaLeighLingerie.com)

Kiki de Montparnasse Provocative lingerie, accessories and 'instruments of pleasure'. (Kikidm.com)

Letters of Marque Inspired by one-of-a-kind pieces like a 150 year old 'combing jacket' and the owner's Dutch pirate ancestor whom, she discovered, had a 'Letter of Marque' – an historical document that turned pirates into privateers and entitling them to invade and keep any booty they found. (LettersofMarque.com)

La Fille d'O Ultra sexy lingerie for sexy fashionistas. (LaFilledO.com)

Seductive lines by Nichole de Carle

Lascivious The first (and possibly last) word on experimental, directional luxury lingerie that is as sexy as it is well-made. (Lascivious.co.uk)

Louise Feuillere Traditional and sumptuous custom-made couture corsetry, bras, bustiers, waist cinchers, deshabilles, skirts, bloomers and loungewear. A cotton bra from her line costs around 350 euros but you get what you pay for. (LouiseFeuillere.com)

Luxxa If you have a penchant for pole dancing, try here. (luxxa.com)

Marlies Dekkers Ever since she graduated from the Saint Joost Academy for Art and Design with her infamous 'bare buttock' dress, Dutch designer Dekkers has been known for Undressed, her edgy-cool line of fashiony lingerie. (MarliesDekkers.nl)

Mary Green A San Francisco treat, this queen of green lingerie is the perfect antidote to mass chains and box store lingerie shops. By adapting and utilising the artistic skills of workers in various countries, her business practices are both ethical and sustainable. (MaryGreen.com)

Mint Siren Embellished luxury lingerie by a Swedish designer living in London. (MintSiren.com)

Morgana Femme Couture If you're a tattooed vixen looking for something romantic or perhaps someone sweet looking for something naughty, you've come to the right place. (MorganaFemmeCouture.com)

Myla From boudoir to boardroom, this British lingerie will have any girl feeling sexy in the city. (Myla.com)

Nichole de Carle Hailing from a line of high-born Huguenots, designer Nichole de Carle finds inspiration in the royal blood of her ancestors, in particular, Francois de Carle who fled to England from persecution in France in 1572. The look is elegant, sophisticated and seductive, with some edgy architectural lines and design elements. (NicholedeCarle.com)

Pleasure State Fabulous fabric, directional design and quality construction makes for sexy, classically pretty lingerie. (PleasureState.com)

Pussy Glamore As a child, Marissa Montgomery created one-off pieces of lingerie as a hobby, which she later parlayed into a thriving business. Instead of waiting for your birthday for these divine and expensive pieces, celebrate now with something from Pussy Glamore. (PussyGlamore.co.uk)

Rigby and Peller A family-run corsetry business, they have held the Royal Warrant of Appointment as Corsetières to the Queen since 1960. They are also expert bra-fitters and can create bespoke and grown-up lingerie at their Knightsbridge, London, atelier. (RigbyAndPeller.com)

Simone Pérèle If she's a fabulous, French fille, she probably has at least a few bras and matching panties from Simone Pérèle in her underwear drawer. (Simone-Pérèle.com)

Strumpet and Pink Designers Lisa Z Morgan and Melanie Probert went on a quest to create the perfect pair of knickers. The result: lacy, ruffled and fabulous undies. (StrumpetAndPink.com)

Tallulah Love 1950s-inspired luxurious lingerie from the former design director at Playboy Intimates UK. (TallulahLove.com)

The Lake and Stars Named after a Victorian euphemism for a woman's skill in the bedroom, this streamlined lingerie nods to menswear detailing, has a delicate touch of athleticism and a healthy amount of tongue in-cheekiness. (TheLakeAndStars.com)

Thierry Mugler Nicknamed Theirry Vulgaire in the 80s, his corset/outerwear looks were ahead of their time then and still look boudoir-ready today. (ThierryMugler.com)

Velda Lauder Beautiful bespoke corsets made by hand in London. (VeldaLauder.co.uk)

Viola Sky This Copenhagen-based lingerie line is perfect for channelling your inner Rita Hayworth. (ViolaSky.dk)

What Katie Did A good selection of faux-vintage girdles, bullet bras, garters and other old-time shapewear. Perfect for anyone who appreciates the art of a circle-stitched cup, a wasp waist or a flash of fully fashioned seam. (WhatKatieDid.com)

Sugarlesque Bodysuits, bras and briefs handmade in London for girls obsessed with pretty things. (Sugarlesque.com)

Wundervoll Since 2008, this Berlin-based label has been creating sexy underwear for fashion-conscious women that accentuates with grace. The style is very fashionista-friendly, directional and modern at the same time, without the bows, frills, ruffles and other details that can make some lingerie tricky to wear on a daily basis. (Wundervoll.com)

Lace luxury

One-stop shopping for lingerie

Below are a selection of shops that specialise in the most glamorous of lingerie and other accoutrements. Visit online or pay a visit in person.

Catriona MacKechnie A carefully edited selection of fashion lingerie including Carine Gilson, Fifi Chachnil, Damaris, Mimi Holliday and VPL. (CatrionaMacKechnie.com)

Coco de Mer In addition to titillating lingerie, they carry erotic books, housewares, handcrafted leather pieces, jewelry and fun bedroom toys. (Coco-de-Mer.com)

Figleaves.com Lingerie and undies for the whole family, including shapewear, glamour wear and vintage wear. (figleaves.com)

Faire Frou Frou Show off in flirtatious dainties from top designers, many of which are simply too cute to cover up. (FaireFrouFrou.com)

Sexy designs by Lascivious

Fille de Joie A stylish source of sexy-vampy lingerie from the 1950s (plus they have a fun blog). (FilleDeJoieNYC.com)

Glamorous Amourous For the lingerie fan for whom the more luxurious and designer her undies are, the better. (GlamorousAmourous.com)

Her Room A good source of everyday bras, panties, thongs, hosiery and loungewear, plus a helpful What's She Underwearing? section on lingerie solutions to various common sartorial dilemmas. (HerRoom.com)

Journelle A new breed of lingerie store with a carefully curated selection. (Journelle.com)

Knickersblog Not a place to shop, but to research your future lingerie choices. The place to find out about new collections, coupons, designers, beautiful lingerie for everyone from virgin to vixen. (Knickersblog.com)

La Petite Cocotte If you want to stop wearing underwear and start wearing lingerie, go no further. The NYC store is a lingerie world icon and they also have a helpful blog at petite-coquette. co.uk. (TheLittleFlirt.com)

Nancy Meyer With more than 25 years experience sourcing some of the nattiest knickers out there, they aim to transform you through the wonderful magic of fine lingerie. Prepare to be seduced. (NancyMeyer.com)

Pampered Passions If shopping at chainstores has left you feeling less than pampered, here is where to shop in an atmosphere designed around 'nurturing the female spirit'. (PamperedPassions.com)

Spoylt Fun pieces for peekaboo and play. (Spoylt.com)

Index

Every effort has been made to contact the copyright holders for all images reproduced in this bo
The Publisher apologises in advance for any unintentional omissions or errors and will be pleased to in
the appropriate acknowledgement to any companies or individuals in any subsequent edition of the wo

6 Andres Sardá, courtesy of XXL Comunicación/12 Alamy/14 Alamy/16 Prince of the Lillies/17 Image
copyright © The Metropolitan Museum of Art/Art Resource, NY/18 Scala/Art Resource, NY/18 Wotan
Farewell to Brünhilde Baker, Emilie Kip. 1914/20 Belts in Ancient Greece/21 Roman mosaic/22 Statuet
of Venus/25 Dior/26 Agent Provocateur, photo by Simon Emmett, model: Kiera Gormley at Storm/28
Les Très Riches Heures du duc de Berry/31 Dior/32 Elizabeth I (the Hardwick House portrait) 1592/34
Henry VII, Walker Art Gallery, Liverpool/36 Engraving of Elizabeth I/39 Photo by Carin Verbruggen
and Ferry Drenthem Soesman for Marlies Dekkers/39 www.gutenberg.org/40 Catherine de'Medici/41
16th Century iron corset/42 Galliano for Dior/43 Eleonora di Toledo/45 V&A Images, London/Art
Resource, NY/46 Robe a la Polonaise, Gallerie de Modes/48 V&A Images, London/Art Resource, NY/5
Alamy/52 The Kyoto Costume Institute/54 Madame Récamier/54 Dior/55 Finsiel/Alinari/Art Resourc
NY/56 Regency underclothes, 1811, *Book of English Trades*/61 Heather Huey Photo by Steven Chu/64
Dior/66 Woman with bicycle, 1890s, www.nostalgic.net/67 New Pathfinder#2/68 Ladies Home Journal
October 1900/70 Corbis/72, 74 Organisation Européenne des Brevets/75 Sarah Bernhardt/76 Eres/78
Andres Sardá, courtesy of XXL Comunicación/79 Panty by Wolford, The Secret Shape Panty/80 Courte
of Spanx, Inc."/82 Corbis/85 Andres Sardá, courtesy of XXL Comunicación/86 Annette Kellerman/88
Courtesy of Jockey/90 Yesterday Girls/92 Nose art on B-25J Serial Number 44-29939/94 Getty/94
Alfred T. Palmer/98 Alamy/100 Alamy/102 Getty/103 Corbis/104 Alamy/106 Alamy/108 Corbis/11
Kobal/112 Alamy/114 Courtesy of FAASVERONIQUE, photo by Carin Verbruggen and Ferry Drenth
Soesman for Marlies Dekkers/117 Kriss Soonik Loungerie, www.kriss-soonik.com, photographer: Chris
Wells, Model Lüsi, H&MU: Shari Rendle/188 Corbis/120 Getty/122 Corbis/125 Agent Provocateur,
photo by Simon Emmett, model: Kiera Gormley at Storm/126 Morganna Femme Couture/128, 131,
133, 135 Alamy/136 Dior/137, 139, 141 Alamy/142 Courtesy of Devanny Pinn at www.devannypinn.
net/144, 147, 149 Alamy/151 Corbis/152 Banana Skirt:Folies Bergère production, "Un Vent de Folie",
1927, www.sheldonconcerthall.org/153 Getty/155 Alamy/156 Nicole de Carle, www.nicholedecarle.
com/157 Alamy/158 Corbis/160 Getty/162 Courtesy of Immodesty Blaize, photo by Simon Emmett,
www.immodestyblaize.com/164 Morganna Femme Couture/166 Alamy/169 Corbis/170 Courtesy of
Robin Whittle, *Womans Day*, November 1965/171 Agent Provocateur, photo by Simon Emmett, model
Kiera Gormley at Storm/172 Yesterday Girls/173 Film still from Anna Biller's *Viva*, photo by C. Thoma
Lewis/175 Spicy-Adventure Stories (January 1935, vol. 1, no. 4) *The Devil's Claw* by Ben Judson/177
Corbis/178 Alamy/180 Ali Mahdavi, www.alimahdavi.net and a special thanks to Mr. Pearl/183, 185 Vi
Les Curves! Hips and Curves from www.hipsandcurves.com/186 Getty/188 Corbis/189, 190 Alamy/19
Courtesy of Marthe Charles at La Vie en Rose for Aubude/195 Nichole de Carle, www.nicholedecarle.
com/196 Damaris, www.damaris.co.uk, +44(0)2076132213, £148/198 Kiki De Montparnasse, photos
by Jenny Gage and Tom Betterton/200 Andres Sardá, courtesy of XXL Comunicación/201 Courtesy of
Strumpet & Pink, photographer: Andy Law/202 Mint Siren by Josefine Wing, photos: Emma Hughes,
Makeup & styling: Gina Blondell, Hair: Hayley Welling @ Cliente Salon, Berkhamsted/204 Corbis/206
Bracli - The Original Pearl Thong/209 Etam/210 Courtesy of Sunny Merry, Ho on the Go and www.
hoonthego.com/212 Maison Close/214 Viva Les Curves! Hips and Curves from www.hipsandcurves.
com/216 Nichole de Carle, www.nicholedecarle.com/219 Eres/220 Lascivious